Karl Marx's

Communist

Manifesto

A Full Textual Explication

BY

D. A. Drennen, Ph.D.

PROFESSOR OF PHILOSOPHY
MARIST COLLEGE
POUGHKEEPSIE, NEW YORK

BARRON'S EDUCATIONAL SERIES, INC.
WOODBURY, NEW YORK

© Copyright 1972 by Barron's Educational Series, Inc.

All rights reserved.
No part of this book may be reproduced
in any form, by photostat, microfilm, xerography,
or any other means, or incorporated into any
information retrieval system, electronic or
mechanical, without the written permission
of the copyright owner.

All inquiries should be addressed to:

Barron's Educational Series, Inc.
113 Crossways Park Drive
Woodbury, New York 11797

Library of Congress Catalog Card No. 73-184893

International Standard Book No. 0-8120-0437-X

PRINTED IN THE UNITED STATES OF AMERICA

FOREWORD

In an era torn by both domestic and international strife based upon differences between those fighting to destroy existing social structures and those fighting to preserve them, Marx's *Manifesto* appears to be just as important — perhaps more so — as the day it was first published.

Its words have assumed increasing importance, not only because there are countries now known as Communist and those known as non-Communist, but because more people have become aware of conflicts between those who are oppressed and those who are oppressors. Whether the parties on either side are black men and white men in America (and other parts of the world), military governments and peasants in other countries, makes no real difference.

The *Manifesto* is a "historical document," but it is also a contemporary document describing society as a battlefield for social and political warfare. Its details are long since forgotten. Its spirit is quite alive. The living quality it possesses makes it a particularly interesting document to study.

CONTENTS

5
Summary and Commentary   42

6
Some Critical Opinions   134

7
The Communist Manifesto   145

1

Marx's Life and Works

Marx came from a well-to-do, middle-class family, was well educated, and married happily. Yet his mature life was plagued by police surveillance, flight from persecution, poverty, personal suffering, and public misunderstanding. He died awaiting the social revolution he so confidently hoped for.

The city of Trier, where Karl Heinrich Marx was born, lies on the right bank of the Moselle River, less than six miles east of present-day Luxembourg. His birth on May 5, 1818, as the second child and first son of a patriotic and well-to-do Prussian lawyer, Heinrich (Hirschel) Marx, and his wife, Henrietta Pressborck, was a celebrated event. The elder Marx traced his lineage back to a prominent Jewish family, Mordechai, known since the sixteenth century for the number of rabbis it had produced, Heinrich, however, chose law instead of the rabbinate, and soon earned a reputation as a talented attorney. Among his friends were many of the city's leading members. A special friend was Trier's Councillor who was also a next-door neighbor in the fashionable district of Brückengasse, Baron Johann Ludwig von Westphalen. The baron's daughter would figure prominently in young Karl's life.

When Karl was six, his father converted the whole family to evangelical Protestantism, although he himself always remained a man of the "Enlightenment." Steeped in the works of Lessing, Rousseau, Voltaire, and Locke, he was as reactionary in politics as he was liberalist in philosophy and religion.

Young Karl was enrolled in the city's Friedrich Wilhelm Gymnasium, and soon displayed remarkable intellectual abilities which his family's comfortable circumstances provided ample opportunity for him to develop. His scholastic standing became a source of expected pride to his parents and the envy of his schoolmates, who spitefully called him "Old Nick." Perhaps because of his swarthy skin he was also called "The Moor." Years later, his own children would affectionately call him "Moor."

At seventeen, he enrolled in the study of law at the University of Bonn. He did this mostly to please his father, but soon found himself attracted to literature, history, and philosophy. He composed three volumes of poetry, and began work on several poetic dramas.

As a result of his literary infatuations, his law studies rapidly declined. In a flurry of indecision he transferred to the University of Berlin, and then to the University of Jena. By this time, he had given up law, and elected to take a degree in philosophy. The universities of Berlin and Jena had been strongly influenced by the ideas of G. W. F. Hegel, who despite his death in 1831, still ruled German philosophic thought from the grave. Marx inevitably contracted the enthusiasm of Hegelian philosophy share by his contemporaries.

During these days, German universities buzzed with

more than philosophical excitement. Students speculated guardedly about revolutionary action and belonged to subversive parties as easily as to eating clubs. They would stage a riot as routinely as if they were attending a lecture. Marx soon joined a circle of philosophical radicals known as the "Young Hegelians." There is a crude drawing of him posing with a group of them in front of a hall. His hair is dark and full; there is the trace of a moustache and a wisp of beard. Who would believe that such innocent young men could be serious about their discussions of revolution?

Like other student groups, the Young Hegelians were under constant scrutiny by Prussian secret police. And scrutinizing the actions of the secret police were Prussia's reactionary politicians. Yet for every student revolutionary banner pulled down by the police, students unfurled a new one.

In 1841, Marx was awarded a doctorate in philosophy at the University of Jena for a thesis on the materialistic theories of Democritus and Epicurus. At first, he imagined that he would become a university instructor at Bonn. But his application for a post was summarily rejected because of his radical political ideas.

The following year he found himself in Cologne drawn to a career in political journalism. As a token of his new-found employment, he burned most of his poems and the drafts of several novels and plays. He joined the staff of the *Rhenish Gazette (Die Rheinische Zeitung)*, and soon became its editor. Five months later, however, Marx found himself out of a job when his paper was suppressed in a Prussian gesture of diplomatic appeasement to the Russian Tzar whom Marx had editorially lampooned.

Still without work in the summer of 1843, Marx nonetheless married his childhood sweetheart, Jenny von Westphalen, who traced her descent to Scotland's second Earl of Argyle. Marx had courted her for seven years. He was 25, she was 29. That autumn, the couple moved to Paris where Marx was able to edit with Arnold Ruge an annual review *(Deutsch-französische Jahrbücher)*. It folded after publishing a single edition, but contained his essay criticizing Hegel's legal philosophy *(Zur Kritik der hegelschen Rechtsphilosophie)*.

In the same review, there also appeared a contribution on British political economy which caught Marx's eye. It had been written by an evangelical socialist, named Friedrich Engels, two years Marx's junior. Ironically, Marx had met Engels previously in Cologne, but thought little of him then. Engels, son of a German cotton-mill owner, now impressed Marx with his socialist views. Their friendship was to last more than forty years, and they were to collaborate on many works including *The German Ideology (Die deutsche Ideologie)* in 1846, and *The Communist Manifesto*.

A police crackdown in 1845 on suspected political agitators forced Marx and his family to flee to Belgium. The same year he published *The Holy Family (Die heilige Familie)*, an attack on an old ally, Bruno Bauer, and wrote the *Theses on Feuerbach*. In 1846, Pierre Proudhon published a book subtitled *The Philosophy of Poverty* which Marx tore into, and the following year issued a scathing rejoinder, *The Poverty of Philosophy (Misère de la philosophie)*.

Two years earlier Marx had come upon a group of revolutionary workers who called themselves The League of the Just, or the German Workers' Educational Society. Composed largely of political refugees, it was padded later on with members of Marx's inner circle of friends, and soon became known as The Communist League.

On November 28, 1847, this group held its second congress in London, and commissioned Marx, together with Engels, to submit a statement of principles by which it might attract other working-class groups. For the rest of the year and into January, 1848, Marx brooded (with some help from Engels) over the metallic words that eventually became *The Communist Manifesto (Manifest der Kommunistischen Partei)*. By February, the German tract was published in London, and by coincidence more than prophecy a series of social revolutions began to break out in Europe. Marx and Engels were jubilant. At least for a while.

Outbursts of revolutionary emotion rocked Europe in 1848 from February until June, and made anyone even remotely suspected of radical leanings an obvious target for police inspection. Marx promptly dragged his family from Brussels to Paris, and then from Paris once again to Cologne. There he founded a version of his former newspaper, aptly titled the *New Rhenish Gazette (Neue Rheinische Zeitung)*. Fate followed, however, and on its heels the secret police. Marx was arrested, tried on charges of sedition, but eventually acquitted.

Frantically, he fled to Paris, but again not for long. An order signed by the French diplomatic minister, Guizot, late in 1849 sent Marx packing. It would be a final flight to London, the "mother of exiles," where he remained the rest of his life. In London, he would publish the first volume of *Capital*, and would help organize the First International Workingmen's Association (1864-1871). From London he would imagine that he was addressing the whole of Europe with the gospel of social discontent. He would dream revolutionary dreams, and prophesy the imminent collapse of the existing social order. His dreams and prophesies were always on the brink of fulfillment, as in the short-lived Paris Commune of 1871. But so far as reality goes, his dreams would die with him.

The first weeks in London, the Marx family was forced to move from one slum room to another. Finally, they rented a two-room flat one block west of Soho Square at 28 Dean Street. Its chief merit was that it was within a nine- or ten-block walking distance of the British Museum where Marx was to spend almost all his working hours for the next three decades of his life.

This émigré period in Dean street was a nightmare of filth, disease, debt, and bad weather. Food was scarce, and Marx looked helplessly on as his family collapsed on the threshhold of starvation. Of the six children born to Karl and Jenny Marx, only three girls survived these cruel years. It is assumed at this time that Marx also had an illegitimate son by his wife's maidservant.

In 1850 his "The Class-Struggles in France" (*Die Klassen-Kämpfe in Frankreich*) appeared in the *New Rhenish Gazette,* and two years later his analysis of Louis Napoleon, "The Eighteenth Brumaire of Louis Napoleon" in *Die Revolution.*

Without work, except for irregular dispatches (at a guinea each) to Horace Greeley's New York *Tribune* during the decade 1851-1861, Marx existed mainly on slight remittances from his friend Engels, now a Manchester factory manager. All the while, he struggled to formulate his political and economic ideas systematically, and to substantiate his intuitions. He followed a gruelling schedule of research and book-squinting at the newly opened reading room of The British Museum which he ransacked for information every hour, every day possible.

By the time he published his *Contribution to a Critique of Political Economy (Zur Kritik der politischen Ökono-*

mie) in 1859, his lot in life had somewhat improved, and he was able to move his family into more pleasant rooms north of Kensington Gardens. His *Herr Vogt* appeared in 1860. But the *Critique* proved to be the first step toward a major analysis of capitalist society, and his reputation in revolutionary politics reflected this fact. By 1864 he had assumed control of the International Workingmen's Association (the First International) until its dissolution seven years later.

His systematic analysis of capitalist society was piling up in detailed notes and drafts that cluttered his living room-study. He poured over them constantly, and in 1867 was able to publish the first of three projected volumes of *Capital (Das Kapital)*. A second edition of Volume I was issued in 1873. The remaining volumes were to appear only after Marx's death a decade later. In 1871, he published *The Civil War in France*, an attempt to deal with the French Commune of the same year.

Frayed by constant bickering with competitor European socialists, and worn down from years of political harrassment, prodigious research, and nervous fatigue, Marx wrote little for publication except "The Critique of the Gotha Program" (1875). In December, 1881, the lion in Marx was finally wounded by the death of his wife Jenny, and in the following year by the death of his eldest daughter, Jenny.

In early March, 1883, after health-cure trips to Algiers and other southern countries he grew worse. He died alone in his room at Maitland Park Road of a heart attack at 2:45 on the afternoon of March 14, and was buried three days later in a nondescript grave in nearby Highgate Cemetery. Except for a brief and innaccurate notice published in the London *Times* (which reproduced the item from a Paris newspaper), his death went all but unnoticed.

Years later, the Soviet government donated funds to replace his simple grave marker by a massive and tastelessly sculptured head of Marx surmounting a block of granite.

2

The Three Worlds of
Karl Marx

In studying the work of any thinker it is important to understand his life as part of a larger drama of cultural, social, and psychological happenings or "worlds" of experience.

First, there is the external world of political and social events; secondly, the world of ideas with its special intellectual problems and counter-currents; finally, the inner world of the thinker's own personality. Thus, before attempting to grasp the ideas of Karl Marx, the student should first investigate certain basic questions, such as, What were the main social and political events of his time? What ideas were uppermost in the minds of his contemporaries? What sort of person was he, and what was unique about him?

The "world" we now live in has much in common with the world Marx lived in. War and riot, burning and looting, student discontent, protest, and political action must remind us of our past. These are only some of the reasons that explain why Marx is so popular a figure in our own day. But we must remember most of all that despite similarities, our world is completely different and considerably more complex.

The World of Events

As the nineteenth century in Europe grew, so did its population and its tensions. These events provide some clues that help to explain the century's major paradoxes. For example, it was a time of great industrial and cultural achievements but equally a time of great social despair and squalor. Autocracy and imperialism were camped next to liberalism and democracy. And across the space that divided these antagonistic positions little communication was possible.

In order to grasp the forces that helped shape the century, it is first necessary to recall some of the central events of the previous century.

First of all, there was the cultural *Enlightenment*, a phenomenon in eighteenth-century Europe which preached the rights of man and the rationality of the universe. "Benevolent despots" persuaded their subjects to believe that their rule was "enlightened." Secondly, there was an independent political movement toward democracy supported by liberalist social theory. In England, liberalism tempered democracy, but on the Continent the converse was true. Finally, in France there was an outburst of social discontent resulting in the Revolution of 1789. The failure of the Revolution led directly to the regime of Napoleon Bonaparte and expansionist French warfare, which helped spread revolutionary ideas throughout Europe.

Napoleon seemed to enflesh the Revolution and its gospel of freedom and equality. But it gradually became clear that while the *ancien régime* of Bourbon despotism was guillotined with Louis XVI and his Austrian queen, Marie Antoinette, Napoleon's despotism was far worse.

Napoleon's meteoric rise but subsequent fall at the Battle of Waterloo in 1814 left Europe a divided, dislocated, and angry continent. The *politics of dilemma* — restore the monarchy or continue the republic — haunted it long after Napoleon's defeat. The Congress of Vienna, which was called late that year and continued the following year, dismissed the dilemma, and proceeded to carve up Europe under the diplomatic illusion that the Revolution and Napoleon had never existed.

But the Revolution and Napoleon had very much existed, and had altered not only Europe's geography but its social and political landscape as well. After Napoleon, European statesmen would scramble desperately to restore "legitimate" monarchic governments, to insure international peace, and to stabilize the state system of government which the Continent had inherited from the age of Cardinal Richelieu and Louis XIV.

Political reconstruction particularly occupied the interest of those countries most damaged by the Napoleonic wars of conquest — Austria, Prussia, and Russia. England, the other victorious ally, began to play a different expansionist game.

Reconstructionism as an international policy was personified in Austria's Foreign Minister, Clemens von Metternich, who became the spokesman for monarchist sentiments, and relentlessly sought to rebuild Europe according to pre-Revolutionary political architecture.

In refashioning the shape of Europe behind the closed doors of Vienna, the victorious continental powers, with the agreement of England, established the Bourbon succession to the French throne. The new King was Louis XVIII, younger brother of Louis XVI. He promptly vindicated Bourbon autocratic pride, for which his country was rewarded within three years with an invitation to join the "concert" of European powers. His death in 1824, and the succession of an even more reactionary brother, Charles X, seemed hardly to cause a ripple on the calm water of European politics. The waters were calmer only because the storm was about to break.

Meanwhile, the idea that Europe could be managed by a *concert* of friendly powers ruling through interminable conferences lost its charm once the memory of Napoleonic terror began to fade. Moreover, the acrid smell of revolution and gunpowder periodically plagued the air. Throughout the 20's skirmishes between police and citizens were common. German universities crackled with occasional fires and riots.

The idealism of the Congress of Vienna developed into political realism and nationalistic calculations. Britain was the first to make itself independent of alliance strategy. In doing so, it unleashed its merchant and military ships into the waters around Europe, Asia, and the Middle East, a move which would insure its imperialistic influence in European statescraft.

A Greek republican revolt in 1830, sparked by an attempted monarchist coup, brought out a new generation of revolutionists. When Charles X blustered his way through the revolutionary upheaval which resulted in France, he was forced from the throne. This was the signal for Europeans to choose between liberalist-bourgeois factions, who favored controlled revolution, and monarchist-conservative forces, who trembled at the idea.

The plague of political change also had its economic symptoms. In parliamentarian, liberalist countries — England and France — economic and therefore social power was being wrested from the old aristocracy by the new capitalist bourgeoisie. In monarchic autocracies — Russia, Prussia, and Austria — social and economic leadership remained firmly held in the feudal fists of reactionary aristocracies.

Liberalism seemed the more humane of these alternatives. But in practice, middle-class liberalism was a scandal to its theory. Behind its pleasant façade of democratic reform lay a growing concentration of economic power managed by an élite minority. In England, the old landed gentry had been distinguished by agrarian serfdom, which bourgeois capitalism forthwith urbanized and industrialized.

In England, the emergence of the new capitalist class, bribing the aristocracy, made its greatest headway with the connivance of legislative acts which it maneuvered through Parliament. For example, large tracts of common grazing land were enclosed, to the detriment of small landholders and the immense profit of large estate holders. Small owners were forced to quit their farms, and move to the now sprawling cities where they competed for industrial employment. By the end of the century, four out of five Englishmen would become city dwellers.

Europe, especially England, was thus drawn closer into the vortex of economic, social, and cultural upheaval. What once seemed the dawn of hope and freedom turned quickly into a dark night of disillusionment.

In this uncertain world of economic crises and ravaged slum life a new spiritual fervor began to spread from England to the Continent. In the city ghettoes it took the form of religious evangelism; in literary and artistic circles it was known as Romanticism. Hidden under evangelical and romantic heroism was growing dissatisfaction with the human condition. Both were escapist movements which veiled deep social unrest. The times cried out for renewal and reform, for the abolition of privilege, by whatever name, and the triumph of equality.

Events were hardening against genuine reform. In France, Charles X's dismissal was followed by the coronation of his Orleanist competitor Louis Philippe, the "citizen king" who fronted for bourgeois politicians. Despite his "liberal" and constitutionalist pretensions, most Frenchmen were still denied voice in the processes of government. Only property holders could vote in parliamentary elections.

In England, the long-awaited Reform Bill of 1832 promised to redeem the grievances of the populace, but succeeded merely in shifting real power from the landed aristocracy to the industrial middle class. When Victoria Regina came to the throne in 1837, few could have predicted how important this new middle class would prove in the prosperity of her empire.

For one thing, the trading and industrial English middle class had to break the strangle-hold held by the aristocratic landowners on the supply of food-stuffs. Naturally, landowners wished to maintain high import tariffs to insure their fiscal control of agricultural production. Prices of food, and thus industrial wages, would be affected by landowner policies. Capitalist employers, interested in curbing prices and wages (in the interest of profits) pressured Parliament into voting a policy of "Free Trade," which meant abandonment of protective import-export tariffs. While capitalist interests in England had finally shaken free of feudal power, popular representation in government was as far from reality as it had ever been.

But the English struggle to increase popular representation found support in other quarters. When the Reform Bill failed to provide representation of British laboring classes, militant groups, such as the Chartists, were organized. The Chartists, who took their name from the publication in 1838 of their "People's Charter," fought for universal manhood suffrage, the right of secret balloting, and the abolition of property qualifications for the vote. Such liberal groups had little immediate political effect, but they were part of a pattern of popular attempts to redress social and economic conditions.

In Germany, the newly crowned Friedrich Wilhelm IV boasted grandly of his intentions to reform public institutions in behalf of popular sentiment. But his heart pulsated with the same reactionary beat as that of Nicholas I, autocratic Tsar of all the Russias, for whom equality was a dirty word.

These events were weaving a pattern which would form the crescent of a new series of revolutions in 1848, the year in which *The Communist Manifesto* was published. The decade prior to its publication had been known as "the hungry forties," and popular discontent was mounting alarmingly. Revolution would dawn when "the Gallic cock," as Marx had prophesied, began to crow. In France, a severe depression hit the economy and the "citizen king" slept in administrative ineptitude. The "Gallic cock" was about to crow.

On the bitterly cold day of February 22, 1848, Parisian crowds gathered uneasily in front of Foreign Minister Guizot's quarters. The air was thick with wordless protest. Guizot temporized. Finally, troops were called in. Someone in the crowd fired a pistol, and this was an invitation to the troops to disperse the crowd with systematic gunfire.

But the crowd raised its dead on its shoulders, and marched through the narrow streets of Paris, inflaming a revolution as it went. The next day Louis Philippe

dismissed Guizot, and the day after panicked into abdi-
cation. The country's Chamber of Deputies immediately
declared the rule of the Second French Republic. By
June another insurrection took place, bloodying the
streets of Paris. Parisians were looking for a "strong man"
who opportunely was already in the wings as the fanfare
of revolution drew to a close. He was Prince Louis
Napoleon Bonaparte, nephew of the emperor. By year's
end he was elected president of the Second Republic.
It was only a matter of time before he became the
Second Emperor. Marx would later ridicule the nephew
for charading the despotism of his uncle. Nonetheless,
the revolutionary drama ended in despotism.

The World of Ideas

The ideas of the nineteenth-century Age of Revolution
cannot be fully appreciated unless we take seriously the
differences which distinguish it from the immediately
preceding era, the Age of Reason. These differences are
particularly evident in the kinds of beliefs that characterized eighteenth-century Europe.

First, there was the belief that human experience is
the same for all men, in all times, and in all places.
Secondly, there was the belief that the "reason" embodied
in the human mind also ruled the course of physical and
natural events. Thirdly, there was the belief that "reason"
not only should be, but was, incorporated in all institutions. Such beliefs bred a natural sense of stability and
equanimity.

But such beliefs had been rooted in a relatively uncomplicated society whose rulers were always delightfully
enlightened, and whose theorists were merely discovering
secrets of reality.

With the mechanization of European economy, however, and the consequent sprawl of vast urban centers, Europe was forced to turn its eyes away from its agrarian, feudal past to face the stark reality of a new industrial power-structure. An era of uncomplicated life had suddenly drawn to a close, and with it the ideas that had nurtured it. Thus, the French Revolution, and subsequent revolutions in Europe, were febrile symptoms of a hidden sickness.

Within a century, Europe had radically changed its ideas. These changes were *cultural, political,* and *social* in nature.

There was, first of all, a *cultural renovation* of Europe's ideas and expected modes of behavior. French rationalism, which had ruled Europe since the days of Descartes in the seventeenth century, began to lose prestige. The Baroque era faded into the twilight of Rococco. French ideas, French art and letters, French science and fashions once dominated European consciousness. In all these fields, Europe had been a French "colony." But as these styles and ideas became more accessible, more easily imitated, they lost their spontaneity and consequently their power of influence. People began to look for novelty and new fashion.

Secondly, nineteenth-century Europe became an arena for *political upheaval,* largely because the once promised ideas of "freedom," "equality," "autonomy," and "fraternity," had failed to materialize. So, in sweeping away Bourbon rule in 1789, France — and with it, Europe — merely exchanged one repression for another. The new freedom in Europe meant that tyranny doffed its aristocratic plumes for a revolutionary cockade. The ideas that gained most from the revolutionary shift of power were those of the middle class whose profits revolutionary theorists had not foreseen.

Finally, there occurred a new form of *social conscious-ness*. The emergence of the middle class in most European countries brought with it dominance in social position and prestige. Below this class lay a subservient majority, the "great unwashed" proletariat.

The interval that existed betwen the Age of Reason and the Age of Revolution fits the later words of British writer Matthew Arnold who saw his society "wandering between two worlds, the one dead, the other powerless to be born."

Where the Age of Reason had cradled confidence and tranquility, the Age of Revolution dismissed both. Between eighteenth-century dreams — where society corrupted man — and nineteenth-century nightmares — where man corrupted society — there lay an unbridgeable chasm.

Rousseau taught that the *state of nature* described man's true condition where once he had lived as a noble primitive (*le bon sauvage*), long before the advent of civilization. But nineteenth-century social thinkers turned from pre-historic Eden to the promise of a completely new society. Revolution meant not a return to an old order (*re-volvere*), but the search for a new one. It assumed that men were redeemed not by the past but by the future.

The times warranted full discussion of the possibilities of new orders in politics, economics, religion, and society. A new openness characterized the era. Emotions which the "classical age" had suppressed were emerging, and given expression in painting, literature, and music.

But "revolution" lurked like a specter behind every idea that called for change.

Revolution was not only a political fact of nineteenth-century life. It was also part of the era's economic, intellectual, and artistic atmosphere. An unexpected form of economic life, the Industrial Revolution, provided a new dimension to the ideological drama. This revolution was distinguished by mechanized production and rapid expansion of trade. Social disorder was its by-product.

In many senses, the idea of revolution became a new educational force. It reshaped peoples' hopes and fears, and schooled them in the assumption that social institutions might forever be restructured.

Continuation of revolutionary work implied a commitment to a future society that would replace élite domination by a popular, democratic association of peoples. Cooperation would replace authority, equality would replace privilege. Rather than idle rich and working poor, there would be a free compact of people performing socially useful tasks.

The spirit of revolution also created the cult of the revolutionary hero who enfleshed all the virtues of 'the future. The cult of heroism infected opera (Wagner's *Siegfried*), poetry (Byron's *Harold*), painting (David's *Napoleon*), the novel (Walter Scott's *Ivanhoe*) and symphonic music (Beethoven's *Eroica* symphony and Berlioz's *Manfred*).

But how were heros made? Here, strangely, doctrines of revolution collided with doctrines of *evolution*. Biological evolution received growing support from naturalists such as Alfred Wallace and Charles Darwin. Darwin's *The Origin of Species*, published in 1859, explained the endurance of life species through a process of "natural selection." This meant that the *strong* persisted and the *weak* perished. What better description of the revolutionary hero whose strength of mind and body assured victory?

The doctrine of "natural selection" had more than biological relevance. It also had social and political implications, and to some observers (including Karl Marx) was
one way of explaining how middle-class industrialists
had survived warfare against the feudal aristocracy.

What particularly characterized nineteenth-century
ideas was their fundamentally *moral* tone. Art, politics,
and even money were all reducible to moral issues. Therefore, every intellectual conflict between opposing views
was a basically moral conflict. This phenomenon may be
partially explained as an effect of the confluence of Protestant ethics and Enlightenment philosophy.

The Inner World

The idea that each man had a special "calling" or
vocation can be dated, for Germans, to Martin Luther
who used the term *Beruf*. *Beruf* implied a life-task, and
fulfillment of one's duty in worldly affairs as a moral activity. Every vocation, or profession, assumed a religious
significance.

In August, 1835, seventeen-year-old Karl Marx submit-
ted as one of his final examinations at the Friedrich Wilhelm Gymnasium an essay entitled "Reflections of a
Young Man on Choosing a Vocation." Like most attempts
of its kind, it was sprinkled with the youthful ideas of a
perceptive student wishing to impress his examiners. But
it was more than this, for it expressed the dedication of
a young man's intellectual and moral powers to his over-
whelming sense of destiny.

Every young man, the essayist wrote, should be aware
of a life's work that shall serve humanity. A man must
avoid the temptations of abstract thought if they prevent
him from *acting upon* the world. By working for the

good of humanity, a man can ennoble himself, and only then will he be truly happy. Only he who has made the greatest number of men happy can be said to be a truly happy man. Indeed, previous history and the experience of others testify to this truth, not the least being the drama of Christ's life.

His words are persuasive:

> "If we have chosen the vocation where we can work best for humanity, then no burdens can overwhelm us because they are only sacrifices for all; then we do not enjoy any shrivelled, narrowminded, selfish joy, because our happiness also belongs to millions; just as our actions live on silently and are still constantly at work, just so shall our ashes be dewed with the warm tears of those who possess noble hearts."

The sentimentality of those words gradually wore away as Marx grew older, but his sense of commitment did not. Years later, he was quoted as saying:

> "Science should not be an egoistic pleasure. Those who are fortunate enough to be able to devote themselves to scientific work should be the first to apply their knowledge in the service of humanity."

In attempting to understand the complex mind of Marx, it is important to take account of different kinds of psychological evidence, much of it contradictory.

There are those who prefer to read Marx's writing in the light of his "humanistic" period recorded in the "Manuscripts of 1844." Others prefer to judge him in the light of vitriolic statements spoken when he was a mature, professional revolutionary and political organizer of workingmen's unions. There is the youthful idealist and the aging conspirator. Which is the more accurate portrait? But it is only fair to observe that the young man was never far from conspiracy and the elder never without ideals.

What is more difficult to access is the accuracy of rival portraits attempting to place Marx's importance in historical perspective. The problem becomes more involved because portraits by non-Marxists are invariably painted with black strokes, while those produced by Marxists are always white-washed. In official Soviet literature, Marx is untouched by human flaw or foible; in a recent biography by Robert Payne he has more personal failings than other men of comparable reputation.

Is it possible to say how Marx viewed his own career? 1. Did he think he was a prophet? 2. Or a scientist? 3. Or an innovator?

1. Marx had few illusions about "prophethood" or "prophecy" — his or anyone else's. But he did seem to be seriously convinced that he was the spokesman for a new age which would witness the freedom of the common working man and the end of social privilege. In this sense he considered himself a *prophet*.

Yet history would both fulfill and nullify his prophecies. In twentieth-century Russia, his dream of a communist society would turn from theoretic impossibility (he never took Russia seriously) to political actuality. In England, France, and Germany, where he expected the imminent collapse of middle-class power, that power increased and spread to lower classes, and "de-stratified" those societies. Capitalist societies were forced to "socialize" themselves. But none of them surrendered national identity in doing so. Marx could not have foreseen how in the late twentieth century "underdeveloped nations" would use his ideas to express their own national aspirations.

2. Above all, Marx considered himself a *scientist*. He once said that his scientific studies had been interrupted

only during the period 1844-1857 when he devoted himself to radical journalism and political action.

Drawing upon the insights of British economists, Marx believed that he had strengthened political economy as a science, and brought it new rigor. As early as the "Manuscripts of 1844" we find evidence that Marx was engaged in purely "scientific" work. There he had written the following words:

> "We have proceeded from the presuppositions of political economy. We have accepted its language and its laws. We presupposed private property, the separation of labor, capital, and land, and hence of wages, profit or capital, and rent; likewise the division of labor, competition, the concept of exchange value, etc. From political economy itself, in its own words, we have shown that the worker sinks to the level of a commodity, the most miserable commodity; that the misery of the worker is inversely proportional to the power and volume of his production; that the necessary result of competition is the accumulation of capital in a few hands and thus the revival of monopolies in a more frightful form; and finally that the distinction between capitalist and landowner, between agricultural labor and industrial worker, disappears and the whole society must divide into the two classes of *proprietors* and propertyless *workers*."

Thus, early in his career, Marx had laid the foundations of the ideas on which he would build in his later works. As a *scientist*, Marx assumed that he was merely working out the descriptive implications of the material laws of the society in which he lived.

Engels once wrote that with Marx "Socialism became a science," meaning that socialism was no longer a utopian dream. And then Engels suggested Marx's two great "scientific" contributions: First, said Engels, Marx revolu-

tionized the conception of world history and the materialist basis of all historical movement. For socialism, this
conception of history had profound effect. Secondly, he
uncovered the real truth about the relation between capital and labor. Without these two discoveries, Engels surmised, modern scientific socialism would be impossible.

Marx himself was persuaded that he was the only man
to have scientifically and meticulously described the
workings of capitalist society. For his own times, this
claim was largely true, but for twentieth-century capitalism — an entirely different phenomenon — it is not. Marx
can be credited with working out the general principles
of a "sociology of capitalism," although he would never
have used the term *sociology*. He can likewise be credited
with working out the general lines for the development
of contemporary studies in the sociology of politics and of
religion.

3. As for the title *innovator,* there is some ground
for it. Marx's originality consisted mostly in the way in
which he *combined* the ideas of others, and gave them a
special coherence for both theory and practice. He was
conscious of his intellectual debt to others, and often expressed recognition of it in letters and remarks to friends.
Still, he was also aware of his original contributions. In a
letter to his friend Joseph Weydemeyer on March 5, 1852,
he attempted to distinguish debts from assets:

> "And now as to myself, no credit is due to me for dis-
> covering the existence of classes in modern society
> nor yet the struggle between them. Long before me
> bourgeois historians had described the historical de-
> velopment of this class struggle and bourgeois econ-
> omists the economic anatomy of the classes. What I
> did that was new was to prove: 1. that *the exis-
> tence of classes* is only bound up with *particular,
> historic phases in the development of production;*

2. that the class struggle necessarily leads to the *dictatorship of the proletariat;* 3 that this dictatorship itself only constitutes the transition to the *abolition of all classes* and to a classless society."

What now can be said of Marx's personality? Two phrases help sum up much of it: *single-mindedness* and *psychological complexity.*

In the history of revolutionary activity, few men have been more single-minded or more conscious of the long-term meaning of their work. In Marx, every gesture, every word, every statement seemed indelibly stamped with the imprint of a sense of the revolutionary struggle between classes — a struggle which he forcefully, and sometimes tediously, described.

A man of great personal and moral passion, he spoke from a sense of inner power. He taught others the art of revolution in the same way he attempted to practice it. Strangely, he possessed few of the qualities that make a great agitator, orator, or popular leader. He was often politically inept in dealing with friends and allies, and it is really surprising that he could wield the power he often did.

Publicly, he appeared immune to criticism, but inwardly he was stung by it. Confident in bearing, strong-willed in decision, devious in matters that did not affect his friends, he never forgave those who crossed him. Like his younger contemporary Sigmund Freud, he eagerly collected disciples, but dropped them as soon as they voiced independent opinions.

If apparently insensitive to the feelings of those he knew or worked with, he anguished over the sufferings of the abstract proletariat. Those who knew him intimately praised him for his simplicity and charm, but sometimes privately resented his overbearing ways, intolerance, and unfeigned egotism.

His tongue was sharp, easily tempted to sarcasm and abusive rhetoric. But he was naturally attracted to the ideals of comradeship, loyalty, and devotion. Aggressive, arrogant, authoritarian, he could also be the soul of humane feeling.

What Marx pretended to be and what he acted like; what he believed in and what he *said* he believed in were often at odds. So often unselfish himself, he still believed that all men are basically selfish and act from selfish motives. Was it sheeer ambition that led him to keep his family in poverty? Yet one of his daughters assures us otherwise.

Tempted by mystical intuitions that mankind would be redeemed through good will, he still mistrusted most men he met, and dismissed them once they were no longer useful. He was a man of *this* world, and a pilgrim in an as-yet-unrealized one. He loved worldly eminence, comfort, and ease, and yet chose to live in a monastery of study and solitude.

A leonine figure, feared by Prussian and French bureaucrats, as well as by fellow-conspirators, Marx could bellow and rage like few other men of his day. He believed in himself but not in "Marxism," and is said on one occasion to have denied that he ever was one *(Ce qu'il y a de certain, c'est que moi, je ne suis pas Marxiste).*

In his family circle and with a few favored friends, he was tender and gentle. The poet Heinrich Heine once observed that "Marx is the tenderest, gentlest man I have ever known." But Marx was also a conspirator and revolutionist. Engels remarked in 1883 over a fresh-dug grave: "Before all else, Marx was a revolutionary. Few men even fought with so much passion." He added that Marx was "the best hated and most calumniated man of his time" who died "beloved, revered, and mourned by millions of revolutionary fellow workers."

3

The Sources of Marx's Ideas

Three separate strands of European intellectual tradition are woven together in Marx's thought. These are 1. German idealist philosophy; 2. French socialist ideas; and 3. British classical economics.
Let us consider each of these in so far as they influenced Marx's thinking.

German Idealist Philosophy

The movement in German philosophy known as "Idealism" asserts that *Spirit* is "realer" than *Matter*. Although Kant is its progenitor, and influenced such practitoners as Johann Gottlieb Fichte and Friedrich von Schelling, its most important spokesman is Georg Wilhelm Friedrich Hegel.

To say that Marx's work can be understood only as a complete rejection of everything Hegel taught is less important than to observe that Marx used Hegelian insights and techniques to his own advantage.

By the time Marx was born, Hegel had already achieved international recognition. He had culminated the development of early modern philosophy from René Descartes to Immanuel Kant, which was concerned with employing deductive logical systems to answer two questions: 1) What is reality?, 2) What is knowledge?

A special relation betwen these two questions was suggested by Kant, who distinguished between what the mind could know *scientifically,* and what was hidden from it. Empirical or sense-objects *(phenomena)* could be known *scientifically,* but realities themselves *(noumena)* were hidden from scientific investigation. This distinction between what *appears to be* and what *actually is* was given a new twist by Hegel.

What exists at any one moment, said Hegel, is historically actual. This actuality *(Wirklichkeit)* is in a process of historical development fully in accord with the development of human Reason *(Vernunft).* The development of human reason reflects the emergence of Reason Itself or Living Rationality. The truly real is noumenal or hidden but is phenomenally revealed in history. This hidden Real is Spirit *(Geist)* which is in the process of *becoming,* or of making itself actual. The movement of Spirit from noumenon to phenomenon involves the self-consciousness *(selbst bewusstsein)* of Spirit. What is called "real" in ordinary terms is therefore only what is real *up to now.* What is actual has been *made* actual through historical process.

The whole of *history up to now* is consequently identical with the whole of *reality up to now.* This Reality is emergent Spirit or Reason. Hence, every stage of history is also a stage of reality.

The processive emergence of reality occurs in a logical pattern, which Hegel called "dialectic" *(Dialektik).* Borrowed from Fichte, this logic of reality — or ontological logic — consists of three stages. First, there is a positive stage of an entity considered as a *thesis*. Secondly, there is a stage in which the entity is confronted by its direct opposite, its *antithesis*. Finally, there is a stage in which both previous stages are transcended, and an emergent entity, or *synthesis*, is created. Reality is articulated in a repeating pattern of such moments in which each synthesis becomes in its turn a thesis, and the process is perpetuated.

The final stage of *synthesis* therefore represents three different activities:

> First, it represents the culmination of the contradictory clash which occurs between *thesis* and *antithesis*, in which there is mutual *denial* or *rejection*.
>
> Secondly, however, it represents the achievement of a new stage in which something of the reality of both stages is *preserved*.
>
> Thirdly, it represents a transcension of both previous stages in which a new reality is *lifted up* and *carried over* to a new stage.

Hegel uses the verb "lift up" (*aufheben*) and the participle "lifting up" (*aufhebung*) to indicate this relation. Thus, every synthesis represents a stage in which something has been lifted up (*aufgehoben*) to a new stage of novelty.

Looked at from the point of view of *"dialectic,"* history reveals the gradual unfolding of the *truth* about reality. Each stage of reality is a further clarification of the Spirit of Reason concretized in history, particularly in the form of cultural achievements.

These achievements are enlightenments (*Aufklärungen*) which *objectivize*, or *realize*, Absolute Spirit, and thus separate it from itself.

This distinction between Absolute Spirit and its concretizing in history (Objective Spirit) goes through four stages: (1) There is the "externalization" *(Entäuserung)* of the Spirit from itself; this is followed by (2) its "alien-ation" *(Entfremdung);* then by (3) its "self-alienation" *(Selbstentfremdung),* and finally by (4) its "objectiviza-tion" *(Vergegenständlichung).*

Hegelian terms and ideas occupy key roles in Marx's writings, particularly the *Manifesto* and *Capital.* While Marx rejected the Hegelian philosophy, he nonetheless once confessed that "I openly avowed myself the pupil of that mighty thinker." But Hegel, as Marx saw it, had gotten things upside down, and his ideas had suffered "a mystification." In Hegel, he once said, dialectics "stands on its head. You must turn it right side up again if you want to discover the rational kernel within the mystical shell."

French Socialist Ideas

The probable father of French social-democracy is Jean-Jacques Rousseau. In his concept of the "general will" of a people, expressed in his *Social Contract,* he postulated a "state of nature" in which men had once lived in common and in mutual sympathy and under-standing. In founding civilizations, men had freely relin-quished their in-born rights to the "general will." But society eventually began to corrupt men and to deprive them of natural equality with their fellow-men. Yet it was conceivable that the "general will" by which society was founded could be revised in such a way that men would once again enjoy freedom and equality.

This mythical, rather than scientific, reconstruction of primitive society had great effect upon French political imaginations. Eventually, in concert with liberal-demo-cratic ideas, voiced by Voltaire, Montesquieu, Diderot and the Encyclopedists, it helped to ignite France's popular discontent. These in turn kindled the French Revolution from which Frenchmen sought Freedom, Equality, and Brotherhood.

There have been many forms of socialist doctrine, but essentially they have all developed during the period of Europe's industrialization. This made more obvious the distinction between those who owned property and those who did not.

To many people in France at the end of the eighteenth and beginning of the nineteenth century, the term "socialism" meant "fraternal democracy," or a concern on the part of a community for all its citizens. All citizens should possess equal powers and rights to determine who shall govern the community. In France, it also meant an attitude of sympathy with the suffering of the masses, a moral indignation at injustices, and an appeal to man's nobler instincts. For example, Claude-Henri, Count de Saint-Simon, and his "disciple" Auguste Comte shared such "socialist" feelings.

Curiously, the term *socialist* first appeared in print not in France but in England. It was used in an article published by the London Co-operative Society in its *Co-operative Magazine* of November, 1827, to distinguish those who believed that "capital or stock" — the value of commodities — "should be individual or common." Those who believed that capital should be commonly owned were called "the Communionists and Socialists." The reference, of course, was mainly to the Englishman Robert Owen who had been attempting to establish cooperative settlements (at that moment, indeed, he was in the United States). Owen always used the term "social" to mean "cooperative."

French social theory also gave birth to the idea of

"communism." The term *communism* signifies a revolutionary belief in the overthrow of "bourgeois" institutions and power. It is an offshoot of French Socialist ideas, and traces back to the radical wing of the French revolutionaries who preached an extreme form of democracy and egalitarianism. François-Noël Babeuf and Filippo Buonarroti, Etienne Cabet and Louis-Auguste Blanqui are ancestors of French "communism."

After 1830, the doctrine of communism began to spread among the German working classes living in Paris. "Communism" was distinguished from "socialism" in this period because it was identified more clearly with the interests of the industrial proletariat. All communists were socialists, but not all socialists were communists.

Between 1830 and 1870 the term "communism" signified a subdivision of French socialism. Marx entitled his tract *Communist* because he belonged to a radical wing of a European socialistic movement. Later on, the nomenclature would become even more involved with the introduction of such terms as "anarchism" and "libertarian socialism."

To the Parisian workers of the 1840's, for example, "communism" probably meant nothing more than the distribution of property among all members of society. They therefore did not draw any clear lines between the terms "communism" and "socialism." By the 1860's however, "communism" had lost the essentially *political* meaning it had possessed in 1848.

For Karl Marx, socialist-communist ideas possessed two characteristics. They first involved a *practical* program of reforming society. This meaning he expressed (1844) in the famous *Economic-Philosophical Manuscripts:*

> "Communism is the *positive* abolition of *private property*, of human self-alienation, and thus the real

appropriation of *human* nature, through and for man. It is therefore the return of man to himself as a *social,* that is, really human being, a complete and conscious return which assimilates all the wealth of previous development."

Secondly, socialist-communist ideas also implied for him a *theoretical* position by which the human condition could be understood. In the same manuscripts he stated:

"Communism as a complete naturalism is humanism, and as a complete humanism is naturalism. It is the *definitive* resolution of the antagonism between man and Nature, and between man and man; . . . It is the solution of the riddle of history and knows itself to be this solution.

British Classical Economics

The tradition of British classical economics which dates from 1776 with the publication of Adam Smith's *Wealth of Nations* was capped in 1817 by the publication of David Ricardo's *Principles of Political Economy.*

Smith optimistically saw an economy balanced by the competing and mutually cancelling desires of men in their buying and selling. Ricardo drew a dark portrait of an economy in which certain laws of tragic behavior prevailed.

Of all economists, Ricardo had the greatest influence on Marx since he pictured a world shorn of all characteristics except economic *motivations.* In Ricardo's economic world, there are first the *workers* who are condemned to a life of marginal subsistence because of their own passional weakness to reproduce themselves. Secondly, there are the *capitalists* whose only motive in life is to *accumulate,* but in doing so must compete against one another. Finally, there are the *landlords,* who do no work, make no decisions, but are the final beneficiaries of an economy in which workers work for wages, capitalists connive for profit, while they merely collect rents. In Ricardo's estimate only the landlord stood to gain from any rise in prices or wages. The capitalist would be squeezed out; the worker squeezed under.

A contemporary of Ricardo's, Reverend Thomas Robert Malthus, was also an economist, and a demographer. In his *Essay on the Principles of Population,* he predicted eventual starvation of the world's people if the birth-rate increased and food supplies decreased. But in his *Principles of Political Economy* of 1820, Malthus said a catastrophe could occur if there were a "general glut" on the market of commodities without buyers. Ricardo believed that this "catastrophe" was impossible, since among buyers there would always be a desire for commodities. The conflict in their views would produce interesting possibilities for Karl Marx.

Ricardo's chief contribution to the thought of Karl Marx was the concept of a *model economy* which could be studied in terms of mechanical laws. This contributed to the possibilities of *abstraction* as a descriptive tool.

Furthermore, Ricardo provided Marx with the basic insight that the value of any commodity is proportional to the quantity of *labor* it contains, Marx himself was to put it more bluntly in an address given in 1865 entitled "Value, Price and Profit":

> "The common social substance of all commodities is labor . . . a commodity has value because it is a crystallization of social labor. The greatness of its value or its relative value depends upon the greater or lesser amount of that social substance contained in it; that is to say, in the relative mass of labor necessary for its production. The relative values of commodities are, therefore, determined by the respective quantities or amounts of labor worked up, realized, fixed in them."

4

Nature of the Work

The Communist Manifesto, commissioned by a congress of the Communist League, was a statement of Marx's program to publicize the viewpoint of this trades-union organization. In its composition he conferred with Engels, but Marx seems to emerge as the work's sole author.

The *Manifesto* was first printed in German as *Manifest der Kommunistischen Partei* in February, 1848. The title-page with its ornate Gothic type and heavy border often found on official documents has the air of a death-certificate. It features the motto which is also used as the work's concluding statement: "Proletarians of all lands, unite." Immediately below, appear the German words; "Printed in the office of the 'Educational Society for Workers' by D. C. Burghard, 46 Liverpool Street, Bishopsgate." Late in February, the edition was mailed to German addresses of the "Educational Society for Workers," which were in reality branches of The Communist League.

The work had been commissioned by leaders of the second congress of The Communist League during a ten-day meeting in London in November-December, 1847.

Marx had laid before the group a theoretical and practical program that was approved by members of the congress. A majority voted to appoint Marx and Engels to write up the scheme, and the Central Committee officialized the deed.

For weeks until the following January — which was the deadline set by the Central Committee — Marx brooded over the work, and discussed it at length with Engels. It would, of course, contain many of the ideas both had expressed to the workingmen's association which they had acquired in Brussels in 1845. The group had been called the League of the Just, but Marx renamed it The Communist League. In lectures to this group and through the newspaper the *German Brusselite Gazette (Deutsche Brüsseler Zeitung),* Marx had struck flint with the working-class, proletarian message.

Engels had prepared a list of 25 questions and answers as a first-draft of the work, entitled "Principles of Communism." It contained in catechetical form some important points ("What is communism? "What is the proletariat?") and included some prosaic answers to the questions asked. Three questions, however, were left unanswered — those that dwelt on the differences between proletarians and handcraft workers, and on the place of nationalism and religion in a communist regime. Little trace of this catechism can be found in the finished *Manifesto.*

As Marx dawdled over the text, urgent messages from the Central Committee of The Communist League were sent to his apartment in a Brussels suburb, demanding that the document be received by the expected deadline of January 1. Marx had every excuse: he wanted to consult with Engels who had by then returned to Paris; he wanted to revise certain parts. He reworked each paragraph. A peremptory letter from the Central Committee finally warned that if the completed manuscript, along with certain documents lent to Marx, did not "arrive in London before Tuesday, February 1, further measures will be taken." Fortunately, there was no need for "further measures," and Marx barely met the deadline.

The *Manifesto* first appeared in print in a 23-page edition, and in ordinary translations runs no more than 50 pages. After its re-issue in 1872, it was re-titled *The Communist Manifesto (Das Kommunistischen Manifest)*. Although some of its language bears the touch of Engels' hand, it is almost entirely Marx's composition — the bitterness, the vigor, the indignation, the sarcastic flourishes.

In an 1888 edition of the work, however, Engels stated that the work was a joint production, and inaccurately claimed that both he and Marx had been commissioned by The Communist League to write it. This claim appeared, unwittingly, to have been prefigured in the fact that an 1872 edition featured a preface which carried both signatures.

Engels in later years probably knew much of the text by heart, since Marx had discussed each paragraph with him during the writing. But was Engels actually a co-author, as he seemed to claim? What, indeed, was his actual contribution? Apart from friendly support, probably little — certainly nothing beyond stylistic touches. Many Marxists would, of course, argue quite otherwise; Soviet commentators would have dogmatically good reason to do so.

But close stylistic examination of the text would appear to support the thesis that Marx himself was the work's sole guiding genius and single author. Engels was his devoted friend, an author in his own right, and, after Marx's death, a central figure in the international Communist movement. But the *Manifesto* appears to owe nothing of substance to his intervention.

In the same 1888 edition, Engels naturally had to admit that the work's fundamental proposition "which forms its nucleus belongs to Marx."

The so-called "fundamental proposition" states that, historically, the mode of economic production forms the basis upon which political ideas and cultural institutions arise. For this reason, mankind's experience has been characterized by evolving class struggles between those who exploit — the ruling classes — and those who are exploited — the oppressed classes. Now, however, the oppressed proletariat cannot attain emancipation from the exploiter bourgeoisie, without at the same time bringing to an end all forms of exploitation, and thereby closing the accounts on class-struggles and class-distinctions. This "fundamental proposition" forms the backbone of the *Manifesto*.

In adding substance to this view, Marx rehearses the evolution which brought the bourgeoisie into power. But the bourgeoisie would like the clock to be stopped.

> "The selfish misconception that induces you to transform into eternal laws of nature and reason, the social forms springing from your present mode of production and from property — . . . this misconception you share with every ruling class that has preceded you."

Dramatizing the push-and-pull of social evolution between oppressors and oppressed, Marx reasons that such evolution has reached its final crystallization in the confrontation of the bourgeoisie and the proletariat. The situation is intolerable, he asserts. Indeed, the whole relationship between these groups has become thoroughly unnatural and dehumanized.

What haunts Europe, Marx states, half seriously and half satirically, is the image of those who symbolize the rights and dignity of the proletariat, namely, the communists. The proletariat as he put it in his *Contribution to a Critique of the Hegelian Philosophy of Law (Zur Kritik der hegelschen Rechtsphilosophie)*, "will reorganize the conditions of human existence upon the basis of human freedom."

But the proletariat is not yet a coherently organized entity, since the same struggle that characterizes all human society is also to be found within its ranks. This is why workers continue to allow themselves to be exploited. Competing against one another, they cannot adequately struggle against their masters. Rather than starve, they make the best possible wage bargains they can. But in so doing, they create "surplus value" which is returned not to them but, because of "materialistic relations between persons and social relations between things" (as he says elsewhere), is handed over in the form of *capital* to the bourgeoisie.

The *Manifesto* suggests two problems which could later find more adequate treatment in other works, particularly *Capital*. These concern the self-consciousness of the proletariat and the feasibility of a "classless state."

In the first place, how can the proletariat know when to reorganize industry for the benefit of its own members, and what means should be taken to insure this reorganization? Marx answers these questions as any prophet would. He shows that the future is simply a reflection of the past. Class struggle has always existed and has followed certain patterns. Now the time is ripe for these patterns to be reproduced. But they can be reproduced only when the proletariat becomes *conscious* of its proper destiny, and aware of the principles by which it is to be led to new social possibilities — moving first from a proletarian revolution to a proletarian dictatorship, then to a "classless society," and finally to a "stateless society."

In the second place how can a classless state of mere individuals exist without an organization to which individuals belong? Marx answers this by suggesting that each person's natural desire, once all class distinctions are eradicated, will be to contribute to the good of society. Common ownership of industrial power will make impossible private ownership of power, and hence eradicate strife. Common ownership of economic production will result in productive abundance, at which point each one will be expected to produce according to his abilities, and will be rewarded according to his needs.

Marx thus envisions (*Manifesto*, II) that in place of the old bourgeois scheme, "with its classes and class antagonisms, we shall have an association in which the free development of each is the condition for the free development of all."

Little wonder then, Marx concludes, that communists should now emerge from their underground existence.

> "The communists disdain to conceal their views and aims. They openly declare that their ends can be attained only by the forcible overthrow of all existing social conditions. Let the ruling classes tremble at a communistic revolution. The proletarians have nothing to lose but their chains. They have a world to win."

The ringing call of the *Manifesto*'s final words, which would otherwise seem out of place, follows ineluctably: "Working men of all countries: Unite."

The *Manifesto* is a kind of watershed in Marx's political and literary career. In it are combined his youthful, insurrectionist-conspirational ideas and his later "scientific analysis." It is a work of poetic drama. In it, he does not yet call his view *materialist-critical socialism* which he distinguished from the "Utopian-Critical Socialism" treated in the last part of this work. And yet the work smacks of certain "utopian" characteristics which Marx spent the rest of his life denying.

For one thing, it reveals him as an insurrectionist utopian expecting forthwith that the rabble would grab muskets or pitchforks as though they were storming the French Bastille or the Palace of the Tuilleries as they had nearly sixty years before.

His vision of a communist revolution conjures up romantic scenes of street-fighting, snipers at the barricades, and the conspiracies of Babeuf and Blanqui. But what he called "revolutionary terrorism" failed to materialize.

He spent the rest of his life vainly waiting for it.

5

Summary and Commentary

The Manifesto *sets forth Marx's estimate of mid-nineteenth-century European social life, as well as his predictions of the consequences of the century's social and economic mistakes.*

The *Manifesto,* which runs under 11,000 words — or only about 1% of the word-volume of the complete *Capital* — is divided into four main sections, preceded by a short "Preface." The longest is section I (under 4,000 words); sections II and III are evenly divided (less than 3,000 words each); section IV and the six-paragraph "Preface" account for less than a thousand words between them.

In order to facilitate reference to the actual text of the *Manifesto,* the following Summary and Commentary sections, beginning with section I, will be numbered according to paragraph-divisions of the English translations. (There is a discrepancy of several paragraphs in the German edition. Those who wish to consult the original German text should be aware of this.)

For the student who wishes to get a rapid overview of the work, the initial Summary paragraphs may be read consecutively, or, for a more rapid review, the Schematic

Overview at the end of the book may be consulted. Later, the student will want to return to each of the Summary paragraphs and follow the analysis in the Commentary sections, which are keyed to the full text on page 145.

Preface

SUMMARY

Communism threatens reactionary Europe, and is recognized as a power in its own right. Hence, it should now publicize its views.

COMMENTARY

One of the remarkable characteristics of this prefatory section is that in less than 200 words it establishes the ominous tone of terror for which the *Manifesto* has become famous, especially among English-speaking peoples. Six staccato paragraphs prophesy an impending social revolution and a longer-term world revolution.

The metallic tone of threat and terror is, strangely enough, more characteristic of the English translation — made first by Helen MacFarlane in 1850 and in the "authorized version" of 1888 by Samuel Moore — than of the original German which Marx wrote.

The first of these short prefatory paragraphs, for example, might literally be translated: "A ghost goes about in Europe — the ghost of communism *(Ein Gespenst geht um in Europa — das Gespenst des Kommunismus)*. The English translation is considerably more ominous — perhaps because these well-known lines have now become indelibly etched in our consciousness: "A specter is haunting Europe — the specter of communism."

The English translation, moreover, often appears more eloquent than the original German. The line following, for instance, reads something like this in literal German: "All the forces of ancient Europe have combined themselves into a holy pursuit of this ghost." The English translation reads: "All the powers of old Europe have entered into a holy alliance to exorcise this specter."

Incidentally, the translation also takes a dramatic liberty or two. Thus, where the original text in this preface speaks simply about "German policemen," the translation changes this to read "German police spies."

Thus, Marx's German prefatory statements are simple, declarative, almost prosaic. In English, they have gained in pictorial power. This does not mean that the work as a whole lacks Marx's peculiar gifts of drama or poetic vigor. Indeed, sometimes his analogies are so piercing, his language filled with such passion that no translation can do him justice. It does mean, however, that this most famous introductory passage — so often quoted among English-speaking peoples, many of whom have rarely read further — possesses a peculiar fascination, like the hypnotic glance of a King Cobra.

How can this be accounted for? The events of the past century in Europe, and particularly of the last fifty in Russia may explain it to some extent. Furthermore, these words have come to mean for Anglo-Americans a threat to liberal-democratic ideals.

In indicating the members of this "holy alliance," Marx chooses the most famous conservative spokesmen of his day, men who needed no further identification than their names: Pope, Tsar, Metternich, Guizot, "French radicals," and German police.

The *Pope* was Pius IX, often called *Pio Nono*, who had been elected to the papacy in 1846 as a candidate of "liberalist" cardinals. The "liberal pontiff," however, soon showed his hand as an arch-reactionary. He waited until December, 1864, before publishing his conservative views in the encyclical *Syllabus Errorum (List of Errors)*, which contained among its eighty propositions an outright condemnation of all forms of socialism, particularly communism. To Marx, he personified the worst excesses of churchly feudalism and religious hypocrisy.

The *Tsar* was Nicholas I, "Autocrat of all the Russias." He was also called the "policeman of Europe," because of his intense desire to see that the repressive policies of his late brother Alexander I (a leading figure at the Congress of Vienna) were carried out. His absolute despotism was supported, as had long been the custom of the Tsars, by stiff-spined military power.

Then there was Prince Clemens Lothar Wenzel *Metternich*, Austria's foreign minister and architect of the Congress of Vienna, which he had designed as a lesson in pre-Napoleonic politics. Called the "Coachman of Europe," mostly because his policies had prevailed at the Congress, Metternich stalled for time: if he could not turn back the clock, he would at least try to stop it. Unfortunately, his policies led inevitably to the revolutions of 1848. Metternich never forgot that Napoleon had sprung from the ashes of the dreaded French Revolution — which incidentally had claimed the life of a dearly loved Austrian princess, Marie Antoinette. Until his death, the term *revolution* made Metternich's usually calm brow wrinkle imperceptibly and his eyes turn colder.

Next there was François Pierre Guillaume *Guizot*, a historian turned diplomat, who after 1841 became a minister of the French foreign office. Guizot was to be dismissed from office after the February, 1848, revolution in

Paris for what King Louis Phillipe (who soon followed him into exile) was to call "bungling." Marx, incidentally, had a particular loathing for the foreign minister because it was by Guizot's written order that he had been summarily deported from France in January, 1846.

The term *French radicals* was applied to those who, at the time Marx was writing, had sought to overthrow the existing monarchy and to replace it with a rabble-republican form of government.

Finally, *German police spies* referred to members of Prussia's secret police who were ordered to infiltrate trades-union and working-class movements, and to imprison any group not openly in sympathy with Prussia's monarchy.

Having named those most in fear of the epithet "communist," Marx suggests that even opposition parties have been called "communist," by both their enemies and their own conservative members. He will discuss such opposition parties in section IV.

So far, Marx has written only two simple paragraphs. From them he draws two equally simple conclusions.

First, communism has been recognized, in public fear and trepidation, as a "state" or sovereign power in its own right (*als ein Macht*). Secondly, therefore, communists should now openly avow their political and social programs.

Such publicity, he concludes, is precisely what this "manifesto" intends to do. In order to afford it the widest circulation, it is being issued in six different languages.

Section I: Bourgeois and Proletarians

SUMMARY: ¶1-4

History is characterized by the power of one class to oppress another.

COMMENTARY

The major theme of this work is pronounced in its first sentence: *All history consists in a process of class warfare.* This or equivalent statements are used at least five times throughout the work. It is thus the *Manifesto's* underlying thesis, rallying cry, and central principle. It is the skeleton to be fleshed out in the remaining sections.

As Marx sees it, class struggle is not only inherent in history; it *constitutes* history. In a later edition of the *Manifesto*, Engels would add pedantically that Marx did not mean *all* history, but only all *written* history. Whether this qualification usefully represents Marx's sentiment is somewhat doubtful, since he himself was haunted by the idea of conflict and struggle as a *condition* of reality.

The principle, however, implies that man is *essentially* a political animal — as Aristotle long ago had pointed out — and hence his history is bound to be the record of his political skirmishes.

What is more fundamental, however, is the question: What constitutes a class?

Marx never formulated a "scientific" answer to this question — ironically, the manuscript of Volume III of *Capital* suddenly breaks off when the same question is asked. Putting together what sociologists and others tell us about classes in general, we can reconstruct some of the ways the term can be used.

First, a class is more than an aggregate of certain members of a society, more than the sum of its social parts. It is distinguished by an awareness of its identity as a whole and has a characteristic "spirit." Secondly, a class has a distinct set of behavioral patterns by which its members communicate with one another. Members of the same class "feel" closer to one another; they "understand" one another better; they work together more easily; they share the same viewpoint about many things. At the same time, they erect barriers against outsiders, or members of other classes, toward whom they act differently.

Behavioral patterns are useful indicators of class cohesion. Marx will refer to them many times, particularly in speaking about the need to stimulate proletarian class consciousness.

The presence of class cohesion and a sense of class identity generally make it possible to identify *which* groups of people form classes and *which* do not. Within the same class, social relations are promoted more easily because of a similarity of manners and habits. Conversely, social relationships carried on across class borders are more difficult and thus generally avoided. The most obvious of such relationships would be, for example, marriage between members of two different classes. The ease with which marriages are *socially* acceptable thus provides a workable definition of *class identity*.

To Marx, the concept of *class* involves a sense of group loyalty, which is derived from a consciousness of shared internal strength and common interests. But Marx adds another and more important dimension to the definition of class — one derived from the concept of *struggle*. So soon as he distinguishes a "class," he sees it involved in

a struggle for *survival*. Many years later, he would confess in a letter to Engels that Charles Darwin's concept
of "natural selection" was extremely important to him
because it "provides me with the basis in natural science
for the class struggle in history."

Class struggle is essentially political in Marx's eyes.
But beneath the political slogans, principles, and person-
alities, he sees something less obvious: the unremitting
pressure of conflicting *economic* interests.

In giving examples of class conflict, therefore, Marx is
actually giving an implicit definition of a *class*. For example, he cites as instances of class conflicts (*Klassen-
kämpfe*) freeman against slave, Roman patrician against
plebian, lord against serf. The common denominator he
uncovers among the ruling classes is their position in the
structure of economic processes. Political differences provide the most obvious instances of class antagonisms,
but actually they veil *economic* differences.

What distinguishes one class from another for Marx
involves two economic facts of existence: (1) the ownership or non-ownership of the property essential to the
means of administering how work is performed, and
(2) the personal freedom enjoyed by the owners of such
property, which is consequently denied those who do not
own property.

Ownership of the means by which a society produces
food, apparel, and other goods, is therefore the fundamental stratifying principle of society. Marx's "theory of
social classes" is in this sense equivalent to what has
come to be known as his "theory of the economic deter-
mination of history."

Incidentally, when Marx uses the term *economic* he
does not always have just one meaning in mind. In his
writings, the term appears to have four distinct meanings.

Sometimes these meanings are combined in a single usage.

First, the term is used *psychologically* as the explana-nation of a particular kind of motive, such as the desire for wealth. Secondly, it is used *technically* to refer to the forces and powers employed to produce goods. Thirdly, it is used in a *material* sense to symbolize land and raw materials, such as iron or coal, which are nec-essary for the production of goods. Finally, it is used *socially* to describe what Marx calls the modes or forms of production and the social relations provided by a certain form of production.

So far, Marx has indicated that clases have historically oppressed one another *in political ways* and for *eco-nomic reasons*. Now he must bring the story up-to-date by identifying the most recent ruling class which has assumed ownership of the "means of production." This is the bourgeoisie.

The term *bourgeoisie* comes from a French word which means "town-dweller"; in German it would be *burgerstand*. The words *burg, bourg,* and *borough* all originally referred to a walled fortress. In the Middle Ages, trading towns had sprung up near these walled fortresses, and in turn protective walls were built around the towns. "Town-dweller" thus also means "tradesman."

The modern bourgeoisie, Marx observes, emerged from a previous class struggle with medieval feudal lords. But, in doing so, it did not abolish, but merely perpetuated, class struggles. By creating new forms of oppression, based upon technology and the industrial-ization of work, the bourgeoisie actually intensified the cruelty of class warfare. Thus, "new classes, new condi-tions of oppression," and new forms of conflict have taken the place of old ones.

SUMMARY: ¶5

The distinctive feature of the present is that previous class struggles have been synthesized and simplified in the antagonism between two hostile camps: bourgeoisie and proletariat.

COMMENTARY

This single paragraph compares in dramatic simplicity with ¶1, and completes the argument first enunciated there. It is a stark sentence shorn of all illustration.

Of the first five paragraphs only two — ¶1 and ¶5 — advance an argument. Together, they assert that 1. all human history consists of struggles between classes for political supremacy, and 2. all prior struggles are now simplified in the confrontation between contradictory classes: bourgeoisie and proletariat.

The real difference he is trying to underscore, however, is the existence of *propertied owners* and *property- less workers*. In writings both before and after the *Manifesto*, Marx recognized (as we shall notice again) the existence of *three* rather than two classes.

But here Marx's theory of social classes appears wonderfully simplified. Only two classes now exist: those who own the means of producing goods — fac- tories, machinery, raw materials — and those who are excluded from such ownership. The owners are the *capitalist bourgeoisie* who are pitted against the "have- not" class, the *proletariat*.

The term *proletariat* comes from a Latin word for children *(proles)*, and was used by the Latin writer Livy to refer to the poorest inhabitants of Rome. The *prole- tarii* together owned less than 11,000 beasts of burden, and therefore could serve the empire only by offering their children. (Incidentally, the word "class" is also derived from a Roman word, *classis*, which referred to each of five groups into which Roman society was divided.)

When Marx speaks of the *proletariat*, then, he has in mind those who have been excluded by economic and political means from every just claim to human existence. When he contrasts it with the bourgeoisie, it is as though he were describing the difference between the legendary forces of Good and Evil. For this and similar reasons, there is a kind of biblical awe that invests his prophesy of the ultimate triumph, despite all present appearances, of the proletariat (the Good) over the bourgeoisie (the Evil).

Of course it is difficult, if not impossible, for most members of advanced Western societies to imagine the sort of class conflict that Marx had in mind when he spoke of the antagonism between *proletariat* and *bourgeoisie*.

Much later, German dramatist Gerhart Hauptmann would write a play, *The Weavers (Die Weber)*, about the Silesian revolt of 1844. In it, he contrasts the luxury of the bourgeoisie with the poverty of the weavers. Says one character, Jaeger:

> "We don't need meat. The manufacturer eats it for us. They wade around in fat up to here . . . Go down to Bielau . . . one manufacturer's mansion after another."

Marx has suggested that the bourgeoisie constitutes a class because it has political power, social status, and economic ownership of the modes of production. The proletariat, on the other hand, constitutes a class because it has none of these. The contrast appears simple enough.

Except for one thing: It is based on the model of an almost exclusively urbanized society, which Europe in the nineteenth century had not yet become. Marx would later make up for this over-simplification in his *Capital.* In notes which Engels would compile for the end of Volume III of that work, Marx makes known his indebtedness to David Ricardo by recognizing the existence of landlords, and therefore of a *third* class:

> "The owners of mere labor power, the owners of capital, and the landlords, whose respective sources of income are wages, profit, and ground-rent, in other words, wage-laborers, capitalists, and landlords, form the three great classes of modern society resting upon the capitalist mode of production."

But in the *Manifesto* Marx has no patience with such qualifications. He is willing to settle for dramatic brevity rather than tedious accuracy. Simply put, society is now divided between *haves* and *have-nots*, wolves and sheep, the propertied and the non-propertied.

Where, however, did the *haves*, the bourgeoisie, come from? How are they to be explained *historically?*

SUMMARY: ¶ 6-17

The bourgeoisie is the product of a series of social, political, and economic revolutions.

COMMENTARY

Returning to the theme suggested in ¶2-3, Marx now attempts to account historically for the growth of the bourgeoisie *as a class*. There is a certain amount of repetition of previous statements, but this is inevitable.

The bourgeoisie, says Marx, first emerged from medieval burghers and townsmen, who in turn emerged from the class of medieval serfs. Certain factors contributed to its growth — for example, the discovery of the New World and the wealth that there invited exploitation. There was also "the rounding of the Cape," a phrase which reminds us of the navigation by Fernando Magellan past Africa's Cape of Good Hope, and his success in opening a sea route to India and the Far East. Colonization of America and the East gave to bourgeois commerce unexpected and unpredicated power. With this power, the bourgeoisie compromised feudal prestige. It also overthrew the supremacy of feudal politics and feudal industry. In a word, it toppled feudal society.

As a result, Marx argues, new commercial markets, opened by colonization, far exceeded the capabilities of feudal manufacture and its guild system. This opened the way for the introduction of mechanized industry. Machinery, under the tutelage and ownership of the new bourgeois class, revolutionized the production of goods, and its members became "the leaders of whole industrialized armies."

A curious relationship shows up here because Marx does not make particularly clear whether it was modern mechanized industry that established the new world markets or whether the creation of world markets revolutionized modern industry. He emphasizes the central event that paved the way for the establishment of world markets because America was developed through commerce, navigation, railways, and mechanical industry.

At this point (¶11), Marx summarizes his argument by stating that the bourgeoisie is the product of a long development of revolutions (Umwälzungen) in the modes of production — that is, in the ways in which work is performed — and in the methods of economic exchange.

In describing the political foundation upon which bourgeois power rests, Marx avoids details and keeps the narration simple — which may indicate that he assumed that his readers would be familiar with the story of how the so-called "third estate," or middle class, developed. His readers, for example, would know that European nobles had been forced by their kings to relinquish *ruling* power. Thus the modern state began to be created in the seventeenth century when political power was invested in the king who governed through a bureaucracy of a special group of officials especially drawn from the rising middle class. As beneficiaries of the crown, such bureaucrats owed allegiance to the king in a way that the quarrelsome nobles had not. Eventually, however, through financial loans and ministerial powers, the middle class came to occupy positions of greater importance. Marx can therefore place particular emphasis (¶13) on the claim that the bourgeoisie has played a maximum revolutionary role *(höchst revolutionäre Rolle)*.

The way in which he portrays this revolutionary role makes it unmistakable that he has no patience with the bourgeois brand of revolution. First, the bourgeoisie has brought to an end all previous patriarchies. But in so doing, it has ruthlessly stripped men so as to leave no other union between them than naked self-interest. What had hitherto been religiously and sentimentally obscured has now been mercilessly unveiled. Marx's indignation, which remains fairly high throughout this first section, here boils over. The bourgeoisie, he charges, "has drowned the most heavenly ecstasies of religious fervor, of chivalrous enthusiasm, of philistine sentimentalism in the icy waters [*eiskalten Wasser*] of egotistical calculation."

It is interesting to note that Marx in this passage appears almost sympathetic to the patriarchal relations of feudal society which he had previously characterized as one of the villains in the history of class warfare. But he cannot resist the contrast between a feudal class that exploited by religious, military, and sentimental devices, and a bourgeois class that indecently follows the path of open and provocative exploitation. The bourgeoisie has altered every previous personal relation between man and man into the relation of cash payment *(bare Zahlung)* and exchange value *(Tauschwert)*, and has made "Free Trade" its watchword.

The expression "Free Trade," as the motto of the bourgeoisie, refers to the victory of that class in British parliamentary maneuvering over the landed aristocracy. "Free Trade" meant that capitalist manufacturers need no longer be limited by the high tariff on imported grains and foodstuffs. High import tariffs protected the interests of the landowners who could charge whatever they wished for the produce of their lands. Repeal of such tariffs represented a bourgeois victory. But such a victory for Marx merely underscored the strategic importance of industrial capitalists in a "free economy" where mere subsistence wages would be paid wage-workers no matter what the price of food.

Once again, a note of ambiguous sympathy accompanies Marx's description: Bourgeois abolition of feudal supremacy has replaced the time-honored guild-craft occupations by wage-labor jobs. Even the family has suffered by being turned into economic pawns of the bourgeoisie.

Yet Marx grudgingly, if bitterly, recognizes the accomplishments of the bourgeoisie. With some small sarcasm he compares its accomplishments to the construction of Egyptian pyramids, Roman aquaducts, and Gothic cathedrals. The colonial achievements of this class, he suggests, would embarrass the historical migrations of great tribes — the Mongols, perhaps? — or even the adventures of the Crusades.

Having set forth the history and the characteristics of the bourgeois class, Marx now turns to an examination of the mechanics of its life-style.

S U M M A R Y :   ¶ 18

In order to maintain its supremacy, the burgeoisie requires continuing revolutions of its productive forces and social power.

C O M M E N T A R Y

Once again the revolutionary tocsin is sounded. This time it explains not only the origins of the bourgeoisie, but the reason for its continued existence. The bourgeoisie sprang from revolutionary medieval burghers (¶6) and eventually revolutionized industry by mechanizing production (¶9). Thus, the bourgeoisie is the product of a long series of revolutions in the modes of production (¶11), and historically, it has been the most revolutionary of *all* classes in human societies (¶13).

Now, however, a new claim is advanced. It is that the bourgeoisie cannot remain in existence unless it *continually* revolutionizes the way in which it participates in the economic life of society. Because the bourgeoisie revolutionizes the "instruments of production, . . . and with them the whole relations of society," nothing can remain stable.

Marx leans on the point with ominous language:

> "All that is solid melts into air, all that is holy is profaned, and man is at last compelled to face with sober senses his real conditions of life and his relations with his kind."

As on previous occasions, a reader might imagine that Marx is yearning for the days of feudal stability when everyone agreed on the meaning of the sacred, and felt quite positive about the nature of the real world. But Marx is exercising prerogatives in irony. Has he not already condemned the feudal world for the divisions it created between master and slave, lord and serf? Why then do the feudal days appear so idyllic, so stable, so much to be mourned over? It may well be that Marx, for all his love of struggle and dialectical activity, was also revealing his preference for social stability — which, after all, is precisely what the predicted triumph of the proletariat would establish.

But this passage is worthy of attention for another reason, and this is Marx's special delight, à la Hegel, in exposing the difference between the mere *appearance* and the actual *reality* of things.

Repeatedly and with typical Hegelian touch, he remarks on the difference between how things look and how in reality they are *underneath the surface*. Thus, noble ideals (he seems to be saying) are nothing other than veiled illustrations of the historical exploitation of man by man. The reader need only be reminded of the beginning of the work (¶1) in which the "reality-principle" of history was proclaimed: All history is the record of class warfare. But is it not curious that, if it is a worthy task to unmask the reality of things beneath their appearances, would it not follow that the bourgeoisie — which has drowned religious and chivalrous exploitation in the "icy waters of egotistical calculation" — is to be praised for "telling it like it is"? Naturally, Marx would consider this an illicit conclusion.

One final point in this section deserves notice. It is the structural relation which Marx says exists between the revolution in the instruments of production and the revolution in "the whole relations of society." The principle upon which this relation depends receives special attention in a later work, the 1859 *Critique of Political Economy*. But the point is important enough to require mention here.

According to Marx, all societies can be divided into three levels of activity. For the sake of illustration, we can call these, the *root-form*, the *stem-form* and the *flower-form*. 1. The *root-form* concerns the ways in which work is performed, for example, by hand or by machinery. 2. The *stem-form* consists of the ways in which social relationships are carried out and, consequently, the kinds of social relationships that are made possible. 3. The *flower form* consists of the kinds of ideas, beliefs, and attitudes of a society — particularly that is, the spiritual "flowering" in its art and literature, philosophy and religion.

Marx called this the distinction between a society's sub-structure *(unterbau)* and its super-structure *(überbau)*. Thus, what is hidden determines what is not hidden. In our illustration, the *root-form* determines the character of the *stem-form*, and it therefore also determines the shape of the *flower-form*. In Marx's language, this is equivalent to saying that the *modes of production* — the way in which work is performed in a society — determine the character of social relationships. These in turn determine the kinds of cultural activities which a society is capable of engaging in. As he said in the 1859 *Critique:*

"It is not the consciousness of men which determines their existence, but it is their social existence which determines their consciousness."

For example, imagine a society in which work is done by the manual labor of a large portion of the population. This automatically means that a relatively small portion of the society does *not* do manual work, but only "administers" it. Such an economic situation then determines the kinds of social relationship made possible between those who labor and those who rule, or between master and slave. Such a society is bound to produce ideas which reinforce this relationship — for example, a philosophy which states that some men are "by nature" destined to serve, and some to rule. Aristotle's Athens provides an example.

If we are mindful of the logical rule that "things equal to the same thing are equal to each another," it follows that as the modes of production determine social structure, and as social structure determines how people think — *ideology* — then, the modes of production determine *ideology*. This is what Marx means when he asserts that in "constantly revolutionizing the instruments of production," the bourgeoisie also revolutionizes "the whole relations of society." (Marx, incidentally, used "ideology" in another sense to mean "false ideas.")

Marx would later expand this theory, but its broad outlines are already evident. They can be summed up in two fundamental statements:

1. The forms of production are the fundamental determinants of social structure, which in turn breed attitudes, actions, and culture. Thus, the hand-mill creates feudal society; the steam-mill creates capitalist society.

2. The forms of production have a logic all their

own, and change according to inherent necessity so as to produce their own successors.

At the root of every social alteration there are, in other words, energies that make themselves known in the ways work is performed, and therefore in the ways men relate to one another. This consequently determines the ideas and attitudes that rule their lives. This view may be called the *structural theory* of society.

Marx has indicated that only *continual* revolution in the modes of production keeps the bourgeoisie in existence. Now he can characterize the extent of that revolution.

SUMMARY: ¶ 19-24

Bourgeois society is characterized by a system of expanding world markets, internationalized production, efficient communications, crowded urban centers, and unsurpassed productivity.

COMMENTARY

The fundamental factor in the mechanics of bourgeois society for Marx is that it is international in perspective. First of all, it is enmeshed in a network of colonization and of expanding global markets. In this sense, it is the direct opposite of static medieval society which was neither expansionist nor colonialist. Bourgeois society, as Marx aptly puts it: "must nestle everywhere, settle everywhere, everywhere establish connections" *(Überall muss sie sich einnesten, überall anbauen, überall Verbindungen herstellen).*

As a consequence, the bourgeoisie has *cosmopolized*

the forms of production and the consumption of goods. In so doing, it has naturally affected world *ideology* since (according to the structural theory already mentioned) "it creates a world after its own image," and makes all nations capitulate to its sway "on pain of extinction."

One further result of this system is the *urbanization* of work, since a centralized population is the primary condition for the centralization of production. The country-side is therefore deserted as people flock to cities seeking work. Consequently, the land is rid of small tenants, and is concentrated in the hands of a relatively small group of landowners.

Finally, the bourgeoisie, in a single century, has created more productive forces than have all previous generations. Its technology has made hitherto unimaginable strides in subduing nature and in wresting from "social labor" new productive forces. All other achievements pale in comparison, Marx seems to say. But at the same time he implies that the general *quality of life* for most people has been shamelessly corrupted. This implication lies like a partially bandaged wound waiting only to be stripped clean by Marx's mounting invective.

SUMMARY: ¶ 25-26

Free of the bonds of feudal society, the bourgeoisie has entrenched itself politically and economically.

COMMENTARY

These two relatively short paragraphs summarize much of the material already stated, particularly in ¶4-5.

What Marx adds to the conclusion, however, is the relationship suggested in ¶18 between the economic sub-structure and the cultural super-structure of society.

The bourgeoisie emerged as a result of the fact that feudal property relations carried over from an agrarian society were no longer compatible with the industrial productive forces that had already grown up within that society. This discrepancy therefore guaranteed the ultimate sway of the bourgeoisie, and brought with it new social and political forces.

Underlying these remarks (as already suggested) is a special set of propositions which Marx recited in the "Introduction" to the *Critique of Political Economy*. The views he expressed there are reflected in what he has so far said and implied in the *Manifesto*: Every society has a "material basis." This basis consists of the tools, the skills, the technical experience, or "productive forces." For any given set of productive forces there is a special organization necessary to utilise them — "productive relationships." The sum total of productive relationships in any society constitutes its "economic structure." This is what provides the real basis upon which the political and legal forms of society are built, and to which definite forms of social consciousness correspond.

The growth pattern of any society therefore moves from simplicity to complexity. This alteration takes place first in the economic structures of society, and prepares for more complex growth in other spheres of society. As Marx put it, all the new productive forces of a society must be completely developed before the old social order perishes. Society does not go from one form of production to another except through intermediating stages. When these stages have been completed different social relations are made possible.

Marx's views here can be summed up into two propositions: 1. No social order perishes until it has prepared the means of new productive forces, and 2. new forms of production never appear until they have been sufficiently prepared in the older society.

So soon as the forces of production in the old society come into conflict with those of the emerging society, social upheaval results, and a period of social revolution sets in. The entire superstructure of laws, attitudes, cultural habits begins to be subverted. The real reason for the eventual conflict in ideas is therefore basically due to changes in the modes of economic production.

Marx is saying in this section that in the old aristocratic, agrarian, feudal society more sophisticated modes of production—industrial production—were being prepared. The rise of these new economic forces—which he has just described—made it possible for the bourgeoisie to replace the feudal form of society. The new society brought with it new forms of social and political power wielded by the bourgeois capitalists.

But this is not the end of the story. The bourgeoisie has gained power, but Marx predicts that historical inevitability spells its eventual downfall. The reasons by which he supports this prediction he then explains.

SUMMARY: ¶ 27-30

But bourgeois supremacy — based upon mechanized productivity and the creation of a subservient working class, the proletariat — paves the way for its own downfall.

COMMENTARY

Everything that Marx has said up to now has been descriptive of the bourgeoisie. With the exception of ¶1 and ¶5, Marx has decribed the origins, characteristics, and the mechanics of the rise and supremacy of the bourgeoisie. The importance of ¶1 and ¶5 — which stated that all history is the history of class warfare — can now be understood as warfare between bourgeoisie and proletariat. The importance of "locating" that antagonism *below* as well as *above* the surface of social relations has also been underscored.

Now Marx can turn his full attention to a description of the co-antagonist in the socio-economic conflict: the proletariat.

"Before our very eyes" *(Unter unsern Augen)*, says Marx, a social renovation similar to that wrought by the bourgeoisie over the feudal lords is taking place. *Then* there existed a disparity between property relations and productive forces, so *now* a similar crisis has been reached in the social relations between bourgeoisie and proletariat.

Like the sorcerer unable to control the spirits he has invoked from the darkness, the bourgeoisie has called forth the demons that spell its downfall, namely, commercial crises. These crises create conditions that endanger, rather than protect, bourgeois power, which is built on *too much* civilization, *too much* means of subsistence, *too much* industry, *too much* commerce. But how does the bourgeoisie respond to the threat of commercial "boom or bust" cycles? By destroying competitive productive forces — for example, craftsmanship — and by opening new markets and re-exploiting the old ones. But does this not perpetuate the crises from which it seeks to escape?

Marx is beginning to tighten the noose.

In a word (¶28), economic weapons which the bourgeoisie once turned against the feudal lords are now being turned against it. Still more, the bourgeoisie has not only constructed the guillotine — namely, overproduction — that augers its destruction, but has developed the class of men — the proletarians — who will release the blade of that weapon.

Always anxious to state situations in proportional relations, Marx sets down his prophecy in mathematical simplicity: As the bourgeoisie is developed, so proportionately does the proletariat as a class of workers develop. But how does this class of wage-laborers exist except as a commodity on the market? As such, it is exposed to all the perils of economic fluctuations.

In his *Critique of the Hegelian Philosophy of Law* (1843) Marx gave one of his first descriptions of the proletarian class: It was

"a class in radical chains, one of the classes of bourgeoise society which does not belong to bourgeois society, an order which brings the breakup of all orders, a sphere which has universal character by virtue of its universal suffering and lays claim to no particular right, because no particular wrong but complete wrong is being perpetrated against itself; [a class] which can no longer invoke an historical title but only a human title, which stands not in a one sided antagonism to its assumptions; a sphere, finally, which cannot emancipate itself without freeing itself from all the other spheres themselves, which in a word, as it represents the complete forfeiting of humanity itself, can only redeem itself through the redemption of the whole of humanity. The proletariat represents the dissolution of society as a special order."

Marx now begins to describe the intolerable character of proletarian life as he sees it five years after he wrote those words.

SUMMARY: ¶ 31-33

Proletarian work is bereft of all human character. It is despotically organized as a new form of slavery to which even differences in age and sex are meaningless.

COMMENTARY

Marx now introduces the theme of "alienation," which assumed central inportance in his early writings, particularly in the *Manuscripts of 1844*.

Mechanization has alienated the workman from the product of his labor, says Marx. Once work loses its charm and individuality — which it possessed in the days of the crafts guilds — it can no longer properly be called *human* work. The reader will notice once again how Marx seems to pine for the days of patriarchal feudal society, which he has many times condemned. But if he has condemned such a society, so much the more can he condemn bourgeois society whose dehumanized forms of exploitation are beyond endurance.

First, proletarian work is not *work* in the traditional sense, but mechanized slavery. The proletarian is simply an appendage to a machine. Marx described this process as "alienation." Mechanized work produces a sense of *alienation* in the worker because his work produces an *alien entity*. As he put it in the *Economic-Philosophic Manuscripts* (1844):

> 'The object which labor produces, its product, is encountered as an *alien entity*, a force that has become *independent* of its producer. The realization of labor is its objectification. Under the prevailing economic conditions, this realization of labor appears as its opposite, the negation of the laborer. Objectification appears as the loss of and enslavement by

the object, and appropriation as alienation and ex-
propriation."

Alienation leads to "negation" *(Entwirklichung)* of the
worker, and the clearest indication of this is the level of
wages paid him. Wages paid to the proletarian worker
are dehumanizing since they are maintained at mere
subsistence levels. Or as Marx puts it: The price of labor
as a commodity in the market place is merely equivalent
to its cost of production.

The problem of wage-labor in Marx's thought is of
central importance, and suggests his "theory of value,"
which is at the same time a theory of exploitation as well
as of *alienation*. It may prove useful then to consider it
here.

To begin with, Marx conceived labor-time as absolutely
unlike that of any other commodity sold on the market
place. Wage-labor and labor-time create more value than
they receive compensation for. The fundamental source
of market value is "labor." Hence, when a product is
produced by labor-time in, say, four working-hours, while
the laborer is forced to work triple this time for the same
wages, then there is created a *surplus labor-time*. This
surplus is the source of bourgeois profit. It is not returned
to the laborer, but pocketed by the capitalist. What the
laborer earns is merely enough to buy food and housing
at the most primitive level of subsistence. Thus, the
bourgeois rich get richer and fewer while laborers become poorer and more numerous.

In the next place, the market-value of labor can be
made to fluctuate, and this opens the way for further
exploitation by the bourgeois capitalist. Lower wages
reduce the worker's standard of living, and this increases
the amount of profit chalked up by the capitalist.

Surplus-value created by the worker is therefore turned

by the bourgeois capitalist to his own profit. This means that there is a time during the working-day in which the laborer does not get paid for his work nor for the value he creates.

The introduction of machinery complicates the problem by making it possible for the capitalist to employ fewer, less skilled laborers for what better skilled laborers might do in an equal period of time.

Thus, an intolerable situation is created. Marx explains it with the aid of proportionalist equations: In proportion as the work of proletarian labor becomes more repulsive, so much the less are the wages it earns. And in proportion as proletarian labor is mechanized, so much the greater is its hardship. The working-day is lengthened, and workers are expected to toil more arduously.

Marx does not hesitate to snatch this opportunity to emphasize the inhuman conditions of proletarian work, a topic to which he later gave considerable attention in *Capital* in a chapter on the working day. The feudal workshop of craftsmanship has given way to factory labor. Like soldiers, workers are massed together under the direction of foremen. Deprived of any measure of freedom, they become slaves of the bourgeois state. Hour after hour they continue their servitude to machinery under the despotic eye of the factory owner. The more openly such despotism is exercised, the more hateful it becomes.

As the demand for skilled labor decreases, so the agony of wage-labor increases. Thus, for example, women tend to replace men in manual labor. In the bourgeois scheme of economy, differences in age or sex no longer count. To the bourgeois factory owner, a man is merely an instrument of labor, and has thus ceased to possess either personality or identity. Proletarian work is, in a word, an utterly *depraved* form of human endeavor.

The themes which Marx gathers here were later woven into what has become known as Marx's "law of increasing misery." Simply stated, this means that the accumulation of wealth is always accompanied by the accumulation of poverty — or in proportion as capitalism becomes prevalent in a society, the masses steadily regress. Marx would put this into a frequently quoted remark which appears at the end of Volume I of *Capital*:

> "The more rapidly capital accumulates in an industrial or commercial town, the more rapidly flows the stream of exploitable human material, the more miserable are the improvised dwellings of the laborers."

SUMMARY: ¶ 34

Even outside the factory, the proletarian is prey to the bourgeois conspiracy, and is exposed to other forms of economic indenture.

COMMENTARY

The theme of the previous section was human "alienation," and incidentally suggested a companion theme — that of "exploitation." Here he follows up this latter theme.

Bourgeois society makes it impossible, says Marx, for the proletarian worker to escape *being* exploited. First, he is exploited as a wage-laborer. But once free of this exploitation, he immediately falls into other forms of exploitation exercised by landlord, shopkeeper, or pawnbroker.

This short statement — less than 40 words — bristles with suggestions about the extent of the bourgeois conspiracy. With it, Marx has added another important stroke to the portrait of bourgeois society. The sentence, after citing "the pawnbroker" and "shopkeeper," concludes with the expression "etc.," designed to leave to the reader's imagination the extent of the exploitation involved. Marx will return to the theme of "exploitation" in succeeding sections.

But first he must account for the historical appearance of the proletariat. He will follow the same method used in accounting for the rise of the bourgeoisie — that is, the method of *historical development*.

S U M M A R Y :   ¶ 35-37

The proletariat is the social residue formed by the creation of the bourgeoisie. Although it undergoes various stages of development, it always remains the victim of bourgeois exploitation.

C O M M E N T A R Y

One characteristic of the proletariat is that its members are recruited from other layers of the population. The lower middle class (which includes small tradesmen, shopkeepers, and retired tradesmen living off small investments), and also craftsmen and peasants, sink into the proletariat.

There are two reasons that account for this: First, whatever savings they have are eaten up in the competition of a buying-and-selling society. Secondly, with the appearance of every new piece of machinery and new production methods, the skills of such people are priced out of the market.

While Marx mentions only the lower middle class and peasants as recruits for the proletariat, he has said that recruits come from *all* classes of the population (*so rekrutiert sich das Proletariat aus allen Klassen der Bevölkerung*). Thus, while he has not mentioned any members of the aristocracy or the clergy, he doubtless implies that they too can fall into the proletariat.

The following section (¶36 in English editions and ¶36 and ¶37 in the German edition) describes the stages of development through which the proletariat passes. The most remarkable fact about this "development" however, is that it does not appear to *be* "historical." Its struggle begins "with its birth" (*mit seiner Existenz*).

In contrast, Marx was able to show that the bourgeoisie emerged as a social group from feudal society where it had once been a subservient class. As a "class" it had developed *historically*. But when he turns to the "development" of the proletariat, he suggests no comparable social origins. Instead, he describes "development" in terms of a *spreading antagonism* between bourgeoisie and proletariat. The proletariat seems to spring from nowhere in particular — or rather seems to exist as soon as the bourgeoisie comes into existence.

Antagonism is first expressed by individual conflicts between members of the two classes; then it widens into a struggle expressed in this factory or in that trade, or in such and such a locality. Proletarians attack machinery, destroy imports, set factories afire in an ateempt to restore the status of the workman of the Middle Ages.

Of course Marx's readers would be quite familiar with such events, which indeed characterized the early years of the Industrial Revolution. For example, the Luddite Movement spread through the Midlands of England from 1811 to 1818, and its adherents destroyed a good deal of machinery and factory property. The movement got its name from Ned Lud, a psychotic who is said singlehandedly to have destroyed two textile looms.

It seems likely that Marx had a certain basic sympathy with such events. He disliked, however, the direction in which such energies were employed. There is no use trying to turn back the clock, he seems to be saying — no use in trying to restore medieval forms of labor by destroying machinery. Such energies should be turned in the direction of altering the *conditions* of bourgeois labor.

Another factor that impedes proletarian progress is competition among the workers, which merely abets bourgeois power. Even in cases of cooperation, the union among workers is always a *response* to bourgeois pressures rather than an expression of proletarian class consciousness.

Then is it not, after all, the bourgeoisie which sets the proletariat in motion? And does it not strengthen its own hand by doing so? Hence, Marx concludes, proletarians end up, not by fighting their enemies, but by fighting the *enemies of the bourgeoisie* — the non-industrial bourgeoisie, the petty bourgeoisie, landowners, and monarchists. Historically, every victory over such enemies is a victory *for* the bourgeoisie, *not* for the proletariat.

So far, Marx has looked at the dark side by showing how the proletariat has been frustrated, alienated, abused, and exploited. Now he turns his attention to the inevitable message of hisorical development which leads to the revolutionary solution of the conflict between bourgeoisie and proletariat.

SUMMARY: ¶ 38-43

Development of the proletariat will precipitate a final collision with the bourgeoisie. Such development, along with new ideas infused into the movement, strengthens proletarian class consciousness.

COMMENTARY

Marx takes it as a truism that increase in mechanized industry must result in an increase in the numbers of proletarians employed in industry. Thus, for one thing, proletarians are eventually bound to outnumber members of the bourgeoisie at any stage in this development. But as the proletariat increases in numbers, it follows that they must increase in strength.

A number of other factors (some of which he has already mentioned) adds to the portrait of the inevitable decline of the bourgeoisie and the triumph of the proletariat. There is first the fact that members of the bourgeoisie are in constant competition with one another. Marx has said repeatedly that such competition merely triggers off financial crises which result in instability; this, in turn, makes wages fluctuate. Secondly, improved machinery makes the working life of laborers more precarious. Together, these factors necessarily inspire collisions between individual *members* of both classes, and more and more take on the character of a collision between *the classes themselves*. Workers form trade unions, and thus establish a sense of common purpose. Occasionally, riots break out. The evidence which points to all-out collision seems clear.

Sometimes in these clashes the workers are victorious, and sometimes they are not. But Marx looks farther than immediate effects, for he sees that every individual collision serves to activate proletarian consciousness.

Proletarian consciousness is also fostered by the communications systems created by modern industry, making it possible for workers in various parts of the world to become aware of the common proletarian struggle. Local struggles can consequently be centralized into national struggles against the bourgeoisie.

It is at this point (¶39) that Marx introduces a corollary to the principle enunciated in ¶1, namely, that "every class struggle is a political struggle," a struggle for power. It follows that the development of proletarian consciousness must eventuate in proletarian political supremacy. More importantly, bourgeois industrial accomplishments — for example, the railroad, which provides more effective contact among proletarians — furthers the formation of proletarian consciousness. Compared to bourgeois consciousness, which required centuries to be activated proletarian consciousness can be expected to take but a relatively short time before it becomes full-blown.

The subject of *competition* has been introduced several times before. There was the competition among members of the bourgeoisie, which set off financial crises; there was also the competition among proletarian workers which served the purpose of dis-uniting them. Competition among workers inhibits, Marx now says, the growth of proletarian class-consciousness, and thus becomes an obstacle to the goal of achieving political power. Such competition, however, will eventually be resolved, and the organization of the proletariat into a self-conscious group is assured.

Already there are signs of success, he says, almost like a lawyer bolstering a case. For example, there is the "legislative recognition" won by the English proletarians over bourgeois politicians with the passage of the "Ten-

Hours Act." This act had been approved by the British Parliament in 1847, and prescribed the time allowed for the employment of factory labor not to exceed ten hours daily. Marx claims that it was *only because* proletarians took advantage of political divisions already existing among the bourgeoisie that such legislation was carried. But in reality it was the middle-class House of Commons that pushed the legislation through.

There is another factor to which Marx can point as significant in the approaching downfall of the bourgeoisie and the rise of the proletariat, and this is the fact that the bourgeoisie is embroiled in class conflicts with members of the old aristocracy as well as with members of the non-industrial middle class. Add to this the fact that each country's bourgeoisie is struggling politically and economically with that of every other country. All this adds to the troubles of the bourgeoisie. No wonder then that in all these struggles the bourgeoisie appeals to the proletariat for help, and therewith attempts to drag the proletariat into its political struggles.

But Marx finds great consolation in this fact since in attempting to enlist such aid the bourgeoisie has actually been supplying proletarians with *political* and *general education*. Consequently, it is furnishing the proletariat new weapons for the fighting ahead. On two previous occasions (¶29 and ¶38) Marx also observed that the bourgeoisie was unwittingly supplying weapons which would bring about its own destruction. The chief weapon was overproduction; the hands that would wield that weapon were proletarian. Here Marx includes in such weaponry the political education of the proletariat.

Marx has already indicated (¶35) that sections of the ruling classes are gradually sinking into the proletariat with the advance of industrialization. Here he adds an important embellishment to this idea by observing that the introduction of such people provides a stock of new ideas which help to enlighten the proletarian movement. In this way, the political education of the proletariat is enhanced. An accompanying result of this movement is the further dismemberment of the old society, and with it, naturally, the entrenchment of the proletariat.

Members of the old aristocracy — he is perhaps thinking of such people as Claude-Henri, Count de Saint-Simon — cast their lot with the proletariat and join the revolutionary class "that holds the future in its hands" (*welche die Zukunft in ihren Händen trägt*) In a statement which bears autobiographical sentiment, he asserts that just as the nobility once joined the bourgeoisie, now some members of the bourgeoisie — particularly ideologists who understand the historical meaning of the whole movement — are joining the proletariat.

The actual language Marx uses here is quite revealing, since it is both direct and simple: it can have only one referent — Marx himself who is obviously one "of the bourgeois ideologists who have raised themselves to the level of theoretically comprehending the historical movement as a whole" (*der Bourgeoisideologen, welche zum theoretischen Verständnis der ganzen geschichtlichen Bewegung such hinaufgearbeitet haben*). Marx would naturally add Engels' name, and perhaps those of two or three others, to the list of such ideologists. The importance of the statement, however, is that it counts as the only occasion on which Marx appears to introduce himself and his co-worker into the *Manifesto*.

S U M M A R Y :   ¶ 44-46

The proletariat is the only revolutionary class now existing. It is therefore marked off from the lower middle class and especially from the "dangerous proletarians."

COMMENTARY

Marx has often suggested the destiny of the proletariat. Here he lays down the principles of this destiny without further qualification: The proletariat stands as the residue of all other classes and is the most revolutionary. All other classes disappear *(gehen unter)*. (But is this not a strange statement from a writer who has not yet told us where the proletariat comes *from?*)

Into what, if not into the proletariat, do all other elements of non-bourgeois society descend? The proletariat, he observes, is the "special and essential product" *(das Proletariat ist ihr eigentes Produkt)* of modern industry.

Into the proletariat there spills the lower middle class — small manufacturers, artisans, peasants — whose members fight against the capitalist bourgeoisie to protect themselves. The lower middle class reveals itself as conservative and reactionary — and therefore anti-historical — even though sometimes it appears to be "revolutionary." It seeks to prevent its transfer into the proletariat. Its "revolutionary" imitation is a cover to protect itself when it must eventually be absorbed into the proletarian class.

Marx leaves no doubt about his feelings toward the lower middle class which he sees as essentially reactionary. Nor can there be any doubt that he is thinking primarily of the *German* lower middle class.

But he reserves his special scorn for what he calls "proletarian scum" *(das Lumpenproletariat)*, "the passively rotting mass thrown off by the lowest layers of the old society." This stratum of society, he prophesies, might be swept into the proletarian movement, but more likely will be bribed by the bourgeoisie, and left to remain as a tool of reactionary sentiment. In the 1888 edition of the *Manifesto*, Engels footnoted Marx's words here by observing that Louis Napoleon actually used this social "scum" to gain popular support for the establishment of the Second Empire. Marx himself in the *XVIII Brumaire* later described the part played by the "slum proletariat" in Louis Napoleon's coup.

It is not clear whether this "slum proletariat" constituted in Marx's mind a *"class,"* but it is certain that he did distinguish its members—vagrants, criminals, prostitutes—from the proletarian movement. He would later make this quite clear toward the end of Volume I of *Capital*. There, in the section treating "surplus population"—which he divides into three forms, *floating, latent,* and *stagnant*—he argues that below these the "lowest sediment of the relative surplus population . . . dwells in the sphere of pauperism." Below this layer he includes "vagabonds, criminals, prostitutes," and quickly adds, "in a word, the 'dangerous' classes." Although in *Capital* he uses the term *classes,* it is not certain that he ever considered members of this group to be more than a stratum of social classification.

But now he turns his attention to the "honest" proletarians, the true members of the "propertyless workers."

S U M M A R Y :   ¶ 47-48

Proletarians possess nothing they can call their own because existing institutions are merely bourgeois instruments of political suppression. Hence, only when the prevailing system of bourgeois economic supremacy is abolished will the proletariat be free.

COMMENTARY

As Marx adds further touches to the proletarian portrait, the colors become darker. Added to *alienation* and *exploitation* there is *desocialization*.

For the proletarian, says Marx, the conditions of former social relations no longer exist. The proletarian cannot be considered an *owner* of property, since he has none. His family is not a *family* in the bourgeois sense of that term. Nor is he a *citizen* of any particular nation in the same way as the bourgeois is a citizen. The proletarian *has* no country. In his life, law, religion, and morality symbolize nothing except bourgeois prejudices of society.

Up to now, ruling classes (Marx says) have appropriated the wealth of society for themselves. But the proletariat can become master of the modes of production only insofar as it destroys all previous modes of appropriation. What have proletarians to lose? They possess nothing they can forfeit; they have nothing they can lose. Their primary mission must therefore be to destroy the security of bourgeois private property.

This is the note on which Marx will actually conclude the *Manifesto*. It is introduced here as though it were the first tolling of the tocsin.

SUMMARY: ¶ 49-51

Class struggles have historically represented the movement of a minority against the rights of the majority. This represents the movement of the majority in search of freedom — a freedom that can be won only with the destruction of the bourgeoisie.

COMMENTARY

To Marx, the term *proletariat* is equivalent to the term *humanity*. He has said as much before, but here he makes it eminently clear by singling out the proletarian movement as a *unique* historical event. Where previously all social movements — which, of course, were class conflicts — benefited only a minority, the proletarian movement symbolizes the yearning of *mankind* for independence and freedom. This yearning expresses itself (and the words here are quite Hegelian) in a *self-consciousness* of the vast majority. Nothing can prevent this self-conscious movement from attaining political power, and thereby dislodging the "superincumbent strata" of *official* society.

Despite the fact that Marx considers the proletarian struggle international, he admits that it is acted out on the political stage of each nation. For this reason, he encourages the proletariat of each nation to take arms against its own national bourgeoisie.

There is one other clue that underscores the note of internationalism and humanity-centered rhetoric, and this is to be found in the summary of his argument at this point. Marx says that he has traced the lineaments of "civil war" *(Bürgerkrieg)* which up to now have been veiled. Why should he call it a "civil war" unless he imagined that all men constitute a single society? And would it not follow that when the *few* range themselves against the *many* justice must be on the side of the many?

But the "more or less veiled civil war" is about to break out into open revolution and the violent overthrow of bourgeois power. What could he have meant by "open Revolution" *(offene Revolution)?* Could he have surmised the impending events of February and June, 1848? It is difficult to say. And even more difficult to describe the expression as being either a shrewd guess or a lucky stroke. Nonetheless, Marx was convinced that some such revolution would become the cornerstone of proletarian political power.

This passage has already served Marx as an opportunity for summarizing his argument. He has shown the moral weaknesses of the bourgeoisie, and has emphasized this weakness by reflecting it, as though in a dark mirror, in the miseries of proletarian life.

This entire section (I), entitled "Bourgeois and Proletarians" *(Bourgois und Proletarier),* began with a description of the bourgeoisie, and later blocked out a picture of the proletariat. It is therefore fitting that it should now conclude with a final thrust at the bourgeoisie, bringing this first section full circle.

S U M M A R Y :   ¶ 52-53

Depravity, deceit, and social cannibalism make the bourgeoisie unfit to be a ruling class.

C O M M E N T A R Y

Marx has already made two statements (¶1 and ¶39) indicating that the essence of social life is class struggle. Here he repeats this principle, but with a difference, since he claims that present conditions are unlike those of any previous epoch. Previously, oppressed classes in a society — he means the bourgeoisie above all — have managed to rise to a higher position. Yet the express opposite is true of the proletariat which instead of rising to higher plateaus of social life are plunged deeper and deeper into a social abyss. Proletarian pauperism spreads like a disease.

The conclusion Marx draws reflects significantly on the bourgeoisie. How can a ruling class, which cannot stop the headlong descent into pauperism of the proletariat, preserve any *right* to rule? The bourgeoisie is clearly incompetent to rule. Unlike other ruling classes, it is not fed *by* its slave class, but feeds *upon it*. In his work, *XVIII Brumaire*, Marx would quote Sismondi's notable utterance on this point. Said Sismondi: "The Roman proletariat lived at the expense of society, whereas modern society lives at the expense of the proletariat." This inversion of principle by the bourgeoisie was for Marx as good as its moral death-warrant.

The question is simply put: How can society continue to live under the tyrranous rule of a class whose existence is no longer compatible with the life of that society?

For Marx, the handwriting is plain to see: The bourgeoisie can grow only on condition that it spread the rule of *capital*. And the growth of capital implies the existence of wage-labor. But competitive labor is already being replaced by associationist, or unionized, labor, the effect of which will be to undermine the supremacy of the bourgeoisie as well as the economic foundations upon which its power rests. Result: The bourgeoisie is now producing its own gravediggers *(Totengräber)*.

The reader may have noticed that Marx has already announced this proposition on four previous occasions (¶27, ¶28-29, ¶40), and will refer to it once again. But here a note of sheer triumph appears to break through. The fall of the bourgeoisie, and the consequent victory of the proletariat, are equally inevitable *(Ihr Untergang und der Sieg des Proletariats sind gleich unvermeidlich)*.

With this triumphant announcement, Marx concludes this first section. Now he must tighten the rope around the bourgeoisie by showing, not merely the inevitable message of history, but the imminent threat of communist activity which is dedicated to supporting the proletarian revolution.

Section II: *Proletarians and Communists*

SUMMARY: ¶ 54-59

Only the communist party represents the true interests of the proletariat.

COMMENTARY

The reader should keep in mind that one of the central tasks which the *Manifesto* means to accomplish is to bring all working-class parties and groups — particularly all trades unions — under a single administration. In this section Marx intends to persuade such groups to accept the representation of The Communist League.

Four staccato paragraphs introduce this second section of the *Manifesto*, each paragraph being a single sentence. There is the question of the relation between the communists and the proletariat. What is this relation? asks the author. His answer is deceptively simple: The communists *symbolize* the proletariat. They do not constitute a separate political party. Their interests are no different from those of the proletariat, nor are their principles in any way sectarian. Their sole aim is to make evident the already established aims of the proletarian movement. Indeed, Marx goes further in his attempt to make the communist party acceptable to different trades-union members by asserting the intrinsically *international* character of the communists. In national struggles, the communists represent the aims of the international proletariat. In every instance they represent the interests of the proletarian movement as a whole.

Communists have two especial advantages over any other segment of the working-class movement. In the first place, they are, *practically speaking,* the most resolute section of the working class. Secondly, they are, *theoretically speaking,* the most advanced section of the proletariat. Only they can "undestand the lines of march, the conditions, and ultimate results of the proletarian movement."

Marx goes to great pains in these paragraphs to emphasize the *symbolic* character of the communist party. One can almost sense that Marx means to imply that something like Hegel's *world spirit* has suddenly become incarnate in this representative of the proletarian movement. He also makes it quite plain that the communists hold both practical and theoretical advantages over all competitors who might have any intention of wresting leadership of the proletarian movement.

This section (II) is particularly important to Marx's own political ambitions. If the communists can achieve control of the worker's movement, and if Marx attains — as he will for a time — leadership of the communists, Marx's political achievement could be great indeed. But the sort of leadership which Marx envisioned would always elude him.

The contrast between the *apparent* selflessness of the communists and the revolutionist ambitions of Marx thus makes this a particularly instructive section of the *Manifesto*.

What is equally interesting is the way in which Marx characterizes the communist party. This characterization roughly parallels that of the proletariat in section I, in so far as the party epitomises the virtues of the proletariat and clearly speaks for it.

First, Marx considers the *function* of the party.

SUMMARY: ¶ 60-62

The immediate aim of the communist party is to heighten proletarian class consciousness, and thereby hasten the proletarian acquisition of political power.

COMMENTARY

Marx has already indicated the relationship between the attainment of class consciousness and the achievement of political supremacy. Section I made this eminently clear. He argues that the condition of political power is class-identity — as was the case with the bourgeoisie. Hence, the proletarian supremacy must be prepared for carefully through the enhancement of proletarian consciousness. Such a task is the immediate practical aim of the communist party.

Marx makes it quite plain that the aim, theory, ideas, and principles of the communist party have not been invented by would-be reformers — some of whom he has already condemned as irrelevant. In section III, Marx will devote more attention to such "reformers."

As the symbolic representative of the proletariat, the communist party expresses the "actual relations" which emerge from the class struggle as well as from the historical movement going on "under our very eyes." The significance of communism is not merely that it avows the abolition of existing property relations.

Marx's readers would be aware that many spokesmen

among so-called utopians and other social reformers were publicly opposed to the inequities created by nineteenth-century property relations. For example, Pierre Proudhon, Marx's French antagonist, once declared that "Property is theft." It will be Marx's intention to show that communists are not against private property but against *bourgeois* private property. His position here is rather ambiguous, and he seems to be very conscious that he could make more enemies of, rather than friends for, communism on the question of private property. Does he wish, on the other hand, to make "private property" a bribe to those without it? Both alternatives are possible.

Marx glides over these implications, however, and underscores the "historical" significance of the communists. They are the ambassadors of historical meaning. How could any other party rightfully lay claim to such a high title? How could any rival group hope to summarize the movement of history in such a grand manner? The messianic character of communism is undeniable. Indeed, the apparent task of the communists is to act *merely* as the instrument of historical inevitability. This is particularly evident in the paragraphs immediately following

SUMMARY: ¶ 63-69

Communists merely want to advance the historical process by which property relations are altered.

COMMENTARY

Marx argues here that, like everything else in history, the relations which result from the manner in which property is appropriated undergo alteration. More than once he has drawn attention to this thesis. Indeed, the first part of the *Manifesto* suggested sufficient details to support his meaning. But here Marx does not appear satisfied in calling attention to these details.

Instead, he cites the French Revolution as a clear-cut event that destroyed European feudalism, and brought about the rise of the bourgeoisie and its eventual control of property. The French Revolution, staged barely 60 years before the publication of the *Manifesto*, is forthwith credited with creating the property relations of bourgeois society. Does this not seem to contradict previous remarks that bourgeois society was founded with the collapse of feudalism and the discovery and colonization of America and the East? Or does Marx wish perhaps to draw a parallel between the "bourgeois revolution of 1789" and the apparently imminent "proletarian revolution"? Such an implication is at least possible to deduce, particularly when the example he uses occurs in a section given over to a description of the role of the communist party.

The possibility that this implication was intended by Marx receives further support from the fact that he reminds his readers that the distinguishing feature of communism is *not* the abolition of property in general (*die Abschaffung des Eigentums überhaupt*), as he has already noted in ¶ 62. The real aim of the communist is the abolition of *bourgeois* property (*sondern die Abschaffung des bürgerlichen Eigentums*). The supremacy of the bourgeoisie since 1789 is clearly what is in question since, for Marx, bourgeois property is the final expression of a form of appropriation based on class antagonisms and the "exploitation of the many by the few" (*Ausbeutung der Mehrheit durch die inderheit*).

Strangely enough, this latter expression appears in the *Manifesto* edition of 1888, and betrays the editorial hand of Engels. The original German which Marx wrote simply says: "the exploitation of one man by another" *(Ausbeutung der einen durch die andern)*. The idea that the proletarian movement was in the interests of the majority had hardened in the intervening years. The motto which Marx chooses for the communists thus becomes: "The abolition of private property." Why, however, does he not say "bourgeois property," as he has just gone to such pains to indicate to his reader? Is it because he sees that the *only* kind of "private property" is "bourgeois-private property"? But then what of land-property? Or is this, too, contaminated by *capital?*

There is, however, another reason why this phrase should be the motto *(Ausdruck)* of communist theory, and it concerns the use of the term *abolition*.

The English edition of the *Manifesto* is quite forthright in its use of the term *abolition*, and perhaps this is as convenient a way as any to convey the intentions of the German text. Still, the original text is much more technical in expression. Literally, it brings the reader face to face with the sense of *historical inevitability* which Marx has been describing since it employs a technical term—*Aufhebung*—not implied in the English term *abolition*. When Marx said that the French revolution *destroyed* the feudal form of property relation in favor of bourgeois property relations—as the coming revolution would substitute proletarian forms of property relation for bourgeois forms—he used this term, *Aufhebung*. Instead of "abolition," he means "the all-encompassing *(zusammenfassen)* and dialectical passage *(Aufhebung)* of previous antagonisms symbolized in private property *(Privateigentums)* into a new synthesis of property relations. The way he expresses this is concentrated in the motto: *Aufhebung des Privateigentums, zusammenfassen.*

The use of the technical vocabulary of Hegelian dialectic in the term *Aufhebung* has been noted elsewhere (see page 29). We can conclude from this that Marx is not merely playing a game of revolutionary rhetoric. Rather, he is using a "scientific" description of historical events. Unfortunately, his intention could also be turned to the service of partisan political propaganda.

The implications of the communist motto are further developed by Marx — this time, however, through the use of sarcasm. He appears quite conscious of criticism at this point, and this may explain why he resorts to such a sophistical device.

Communists have been reproached (he says) with the desire to abolish the right of acquiring property as the result of human labor. Such property, it is said, is the foundation of human freedom and independence. Here Marx begins to needle his critics with feigned innocence: What kind of property can be meant by this? Does this mean the work of the artisan or of the small peasant? Surely not, he rejoins. Modern industrial bourgeois society has already destroyed that—or at least is in the process of doing so. Human freedom and private property? Independence and private property? "Or do you mean," he acidly addresses his criticism, "modern bourgeois private property?" *(Oder sprecht ihr vom modernen bürglichen Privateigentum?)*. The question is purely rhetorical.

Still, there remains for Marx to show precisely *why* communists seek to abolish "modern bourgeois private property."

S U M M A R Y :   ¶ 70

Communists seek to abolish bourgeois private property because wage-labor creates capital only for the bourgeoisie.

COMMENTARY

The central point has now been made. It might be summed up in the statement "Private property creates *privation*." Here lies the fundamental paradox of bourgeois society and the essential inequity of capitalist production. Wage-labor does not provide the laborer a just return for his work. Nor does it create for him "property." Since "property" means "bourgeois private property," which Marx has just condemned, it is a term for *bourgeois*-appropriation.

What then does wage-labor create? It creates *"capital,"* or "that kind of property which exploits wage-labor *(das Eigentums, welches die Lohnarbeit ausbeutet).* As such, wage-labor perpetuates its own exploitation. *Capital* is exploitative. *Capital* grows only on condition that it acquires new sources of wage-labor *for the purpose of exploitation.*

It is not hard to understand why Marx, in uncovering this sinful paradox, should be so righteously indignant. The mere existence of bourgeois private property automatically spelled for him the *deprivation*, the dehumanization, the alienation of wage-*laborers*. Capital creates more capital, and more capital creates greater misery for "the vast majority."

In its present form, property is based on the antagonism, Marx argues, that exists between capital and wage-labor. The statement clearly echoes the theme of class warfare announced in ¶ 1.

But a problem arises. Since the *only* kind of property that can now exist is *capitalist* property, the statement that property rests on the antagonism of capital and wage-labor is reducible to the proposition that property rests upon the antagonism between itself and wage-labor.

It follows that the antagonism exists between "propertied capital" and "propertyless wage-labor."

Marx can now make good on his previous claim that the communists are *theoretically* the most advanced section of the working-class movements (see page 85). He has already uncovered the primary and inequitous paradox of bourgeois society, and has exposed the practical meaning of "private property." Now he can give a detailed account of this paradox.

SUMMARY: ¶ 71-75

Communism perceives the true nature of capital and wage-labor. Capital is a product of society as a whole, although it now rests entirely in the hands of a ruling minority. Wage-labor provides scant subsistence for laborers, but actually increases the power of the ruling class.

COMMENTARY

The argument indicting bourgeois capitalism can now be developed so as to expose to a greater extent the basic inequity of the system. Several factors emerge in this analysis.

First, capitalism bestows both a *personal* as well as a *social* status upon the capitalist. Capital, however, is "a social" or collective product *(Das Kapital ist ein gemeinschaftliches Produkt)*. Then it necessarily follows that only the united action of *all* members of a society can produce capital. The power of capital is therefore the power of society itself, and not the power of any single group in society. Capital cannot rightly be the power of a single class. When property is converted into common property, it thereby loses its class fixation. But so long as property retains its class fixation, it remains a social scandal.

So far as wage-labor is concerned, says Marx, its price is that of a bare minimum. It is allowed the return of earnings sufficient only to keep the laborer at the edge of mere subsistence. It thus helps to perpetuate his ignominious condition.

What communism seeks is the destruction of such a system. It is not interested in abolishing the personal return upon the investment of labor *for the* laborer. Rather, it intends to redress the gross inequities of a perfidious social situation, and to abolish only the miserable character of the sort of appropriation "under which the laborer lives merely to increase capital, and is allowed to live only insofar as the interest of the ruling class requires it" *(worin der Arbeiter nur lebt, um das Kapital zu vermehren, nur ein so weit lebt, wie es das Interesse der herrschenden Klasse erheischt).*

Capitalist society ironically provides for the diminution of the laborer as the direct result of his own wage-labor. At the same time, it provides for the continued ascent of bourgeois power. Has any other society, Marx seems to say, been more grossly unfair to most of its members?

Now it is time to contrast the theoretical insights of communism with those of the bourgeoisie on more far-reaching issues.

SUMMARY: ¶ 76-80

Communism holds views directly opposing those of the bourgeoisie on labor, the person, the meaning of history, and freedom.

COMMENTARY

Comparison between the practice of bourgeois society and the ideals of a communist society touches on topics of basic importance in Marx's vocabulary.

First, there is the way in which each conceives the role of labor. For bourgeois society, human labor merely adds to the *amount of labor* to be performed. It cheapens and demeans human endeavor by embittering those who must labor. For communist society, on the other hand, labor is a means "to widen, to enrich, and to promote" *(zu erweitern, zu bereichern, zu befördern)* the laborer's existence.

Communism thus inherently respects the dignity of each individual laborer, and also respects the products of his labor. Surely Marx has made it clear that bourgeois society respects neither.

The historical orientation of each of the societies also differs. Bourgeois society reverts to the past, and is dominated by it. Communist society envisages the present as more important than the past.

For each, *freedom* means something completely different. For bourgeois society, *freedom* means only the license of the bourgeois capitalists. The term has consequently lost human meaning. It denotes only "free trade, free selling and buying."

The same calculated misuse of meanings infects bourgeois ideas of *individuality* and *independence*. When used by the bourgeoisie, each of these words must be qualified to read: "For the bourgeoisie only."

Communists do not seek to abolish *freedom, individuality*, or *independence*, but only their spurious, bourgeois deformations.

The foregoing remarks have introduced *general* differences of viewpoint which distinguish communist from bourgeois attitudes. But Marx means to get more specific on issues that show not only how theoretically superior are communist views to all others, but how little these views are understood. It will appear at first that these remarks are addressed to bourgeois critics of communism. But in fact they are directed at all possible critics of communism.

S U M M A R Y : ¶ 81-109

Simple analysis shows the weakness of the bourgeois defense of its position. It is ignorant of communism's criticism of bourgeois attitudes toward private property, culture, the family, child-labor, the place of women, the status of marriage, and the significance of nationalism.

C O M M E N T A R Y

This section constitutes one of the *Manifesto's* longest and bitterest attacks on bourgeois society. It is character-ized by the extended use of *direct address* which Marx had previously used only a few times. (for example, ¶ 68 and ¶69). It also employs the *Tu quoque* (*"You also"*) technique of rebuttal. There is no mistaking that Marx's indignation is reaching out for the dramatic devices which could best enhance his case—sarcasm and irony, innuendo and acidulous analysis. His aim is a direct attack on the enemy. It is as though he were reminded in this passage of the polemical ideals—which initially inspired the work's composition.

Here, too, his presentation becomes clearly forensic. He is developing the steel-edged arguments which will reveal the bourgeoisie at its hypocritical worst. The device of *direct address* gives the feeling of a courtroom accusation.

You are horrified, he asserts, that we wish to do away with private property. Yet in bourgeois society private property is done away with "for nine-tenths of the population" *(für neun Zehntel Ihrer Mitglieder aufgehoben)*. The existence of private property for the few is due completely to its non-existence for the same nine-tenths of the population. You reproach us for wanting to do away with what you have already done away with—to your great advantage.

The issue of "private property" serves Marx well in this broadside attack. First, because he has already exposed the inequity involved in both the expression and the reality for which the phrase stands; secondly, because it points to the central paradox which motivates bourgeois society—namely, that "private property" is essentially a misuse of social power by the few against the many.

Like an attorney summing up a case already made quite clear to a court before which the bourgeoisie stands condemned, Marx makes his points stand out more clearly by emphasizing them with invective.

Marx swoops down remorselessly and candidly: You reproach us for wishing to do away with *your* property. In this you are exactly right. So long as you cannot convert labor to your own devices you scream righteously that all *individuality* has been lost. But then by *individual* you mean none other than *yourself*. Yet it is precisely such an *individual* that must be eliminated *(Und dies Person soll allerdings aufgehoben werden)*.

It will once again be apparent that this final sentence employs the special vocabulary of the "dialectic" *Aufhebung* already referred to (see page 29 and page 90). When translating the term *aufgehoben*, we often use the words "abolished" or "swept away" to convey Marx's meaning. But despite all the political rhetoric often attributed to him, Marx is still using "scientific" language. He is not merely referring to some seditious plan to overthrow bourgeois society as staged by some particular group of visionary revolutionaries. He is still talking about the inevitable course of *history*. The bourgeoisie will be ineluctably and historically overthrown, since it exists as a thesis for which the proletariat is the *antithesis*. The bourgeoisie will have been swept away *(aufgehoben)* in the dialectical course of events. The agency to bring about this process has already been selected.

It is obvious now that the communists constitute the *special* agency—the surrogates—of the historical process. Is it not clear that the communists represent the genuine interests of the proletariat? Is it not equally clear what sort of role they will have to play in the "abolition" of the bourgeoisie?

Communism, therefore, sets itself irreversibly against those who wish to subjugate the labor of others through the misappropriation of social goods. It elects this as its self-appointed task.

But Marx must now turn his attention to the rebuttal of another bourgeois argument against communist society. It is said that if private property is abolished, universal laziness will ensue, and no one will do any work. Here Marx has sharpened his retort: Society should long ago have ceased to exist had it been governed by the spirit of idleness which the bourgeoisie has fostered. Clearly Marx is referring not so much to the "manager" bourgeoisie as to the "banker" bourgeoisie. And, of course, he is including implicitly the landed aristocracy.

The fear of creating a society in which laziness could prevail is a middle-class fear, as Marx well knew; and he is here exposing its inner contradiction. Ever since the days of John Calvin the *gospel of work* was preached by the Protestant middle-class in Europe. Indeed, Max Weber would later write a book comparing Protestant morality and the spirit of capitalism. For such an ethic, success is a symbol of God's preference, and the direct result of hard work, while idleness is the outward sign of sin. Along with the fear of lower-class idleness, there was also a sense of *respectability* which characterized middle-class morality.

Marx, however, is basing his argument here on the "idleness of a few." He speaks against a society in which "those of its members who work, acquire nothing, and those who acquire anything do not work" (*denn die in ihr arbeiten, erwerben nicht, und die in ihr erwerben, arbeiten nicht*). The point is rhetorically effective but it is aimed at the revival of feudal privilege. Yet, the rope that hangs the bourgeoisie must also hang the older aristocracy. Marx therefore plays hangman for the former.

Why does the bourgeoisie assume that the eradication of its mode of appropriation is equivalent to the abolition of all appropriation? Why does it assume that the abolition of its own *culture* is synonymous with the destruction of *all* forms of culture? Yet what is the net result of "bourgeois culture?" For the immense majority it is a mere training to act as a machine (*für die enorme Mahrzahl die Heranbildung zur Maschine*). Furthermore, what is the relation between any *culture* and its *ideology?* Marx has touched on this, as we have already noted (see page 59ff).

The argument is simple enough: The bourgeois notion of law, for example, is merely an expression of the bourgeois mode of production. The accepted theory of law in bourgeois *ideology* is merely "the will of your class."

And this *will* is determined by the economic conditions of bourgeois society.

The bourgeois mind has turned into eternal laws of nature and reason *(in ewige Natur- und Vernunftgesetze)* the prejudices of its own mode of production. Laws are not eternal, but are merely the products of the historical relation established by every ruling class. Bourgeois abolition of feudal property and feudal rule illustrated this fact. Why cannot the bourgeoisie accept as a historical, and therefore repeatable, occurrence this elementary truth? (Is this evidence that Marx assumes that history repeats itself as so far implied? But it misses his sense of historical novelty.)

Having considered the erroneous views held by the bourgeoisie on the meaning of private property and culture, Marx now turns his attention to the meaning of the family.

What does one mean by the communist phrase "abolition of the family" *(Aufhebung der Familie)?* Marx admits that even the most radical can become enraged by such a phrase. Employing the same device he has used on other occasions, he takes up instead the question of what the *bourgeoisie* has made of the family.

The bourgeois family has been based on private gain. In a word, on *capital.* Only the *bourgeoisie* can afford *families.* Among the proletariat there are no families; there is only prostitution. Thus, in one stroke Marx has turned the tables by arguing that the *bourgeoisie* itself has abolished all families except its own. When the bourgeois family vanishes, he says with dialectical fury, the proletarian charade of family will also vanish. The abolition of both will be accompanied by the abolition of *capital (mit dem Verschwinden des Kapital).*

Then with mock apology Marx confesses that communists readily plead to the charge of wishing to stop the exploitation of children by their parents. They also wish to provide *social* education for children in place of the so-called *education* that takes place in the proletarian *home.* Again, he brings attention to the *ideals* of bourgeois education as opposed to the reality of "industrial culture." Just compare the relations between parent and child as they are piously recited by the bourgeoisie with the actual conditions that prevail. The claptrap *(Redensarten)* which the bourgeoisie parades abroad about the holiness of family life is betrayed by the very conditions of industrial society. *There* most children are not sacred, but a most unholy breed ripped by the cutting edge of modern industrial conditions. He knew of the practice, common in England, of hiring out whole wards of orphans to work in industrial mills. Often the children were chained to the machinery, and worked up to 14 hours a day.

The next charge Marx must answer concerns not family life so much as marriage and the place of women in society. Here his use of the rhetorical device known as *Tu quoque* ("You do it too") is once again in evidence. Its effect is intensified by mockery.

The whole chorus of bourgeois acolytes screams in indignation that communists would inaugurate a *community of women.* But does not every bourgeois man see in his wife a mere instrument of production—for the creation of children? Naturally then, the bourgeois assumes that wives must be exploited. Has he himself not exploited everything he has touched? Has he not also heard that communists wish to communalize the modes of production? Here Marx's conclusion is venomously extracted: Would it not follow for such a mind that women must be used in common by all? But never does it occur to such a person that the whole point of the communist position is to do away with the very concept of exploitation—particularly the exploitation of women.

Together with Engels in an earlier work, *The Holy Family*, Marx had made known his criticism of the way in which *civilization* continues to debase the position of women. Referring particularly to bourgeois civilization he argued there that the bourgeois *family* perpetuates adultery and seduction, and contrasted this with the habits of *barbaric* societies. He put it this way:

> "The debasement of the female sex is an essential character trait of civilization no less than of barbarism with this difference, that under civilization all the vices which barbarism practices in a simple and straightforward way are now preserved in a complicated, ambiguous, hypocritical semblance."

Marx's venom, once drawn, begins to flow more freely: Does the bourgeois critic believe that communists try to communalize women when each knows full well that female communalization has existed from the very beginning of bourgeois society? The bourgeois gentleman, apart from having at his disposal the wives and daughters of proletarians—and common prostitutes as well—delight in seducing each other's wives. Marx's conclusion rings with righteousness: Indeed, what is bourgeois marriage except a way of having a series of wives in common? At most, communists would substitute an un-hypocritical community of wives. With the collapse of bourgeois appropriation the bourgeois community of women, and the system of public and private prostitution, must also collapse. Thus, with a flourish of moral indignation and

sophistical argument Marx turns to the issues of nationalism.

The reader should recall that to mid-nineteenth-century Europe, about to witness the unification of Italy and
Germany, the question of national identity was of tre-
mendous importance. Marx must therefore put forward
a competitive identity if he is to make his case. Do communists seek to topple countries and nations? But workingmen have no country, rejoins Marx; so "no one can
take from them what they have not got" (Man kann ihnen
nicht nehmen, was sie nicht haben). Therefore, he argues,
the proletariat itself must become the only "nation" deserving the name.

Furthermore, Marx observes, nationalism is already
vanishing as the interests of the bourgeoisie increase.
With the rise to power of the *proletariat* should not nationalism vanish more rapidly? Marx seems to follow the
argument wherever it leads. Is not one of the conditions
for emancipating the proletariat the success of "united
action" (Vereinigte Aktion) among leading nations of the
world? What precisely he means by "united action" is
somewhat hazy; but it is clear that in some way he is
speaking of *proletarian* union.

The argument is complicated, however, by the introduction of the notion that exploitation will one day decline.
In proportion as individual exploitation ceases, so too
will one nation cease to exploit another. And in proportion as class antagonisms *within* nations cease, so too
will antagonisms *between* nations vanish. It all seems
so simple a process to Marx. Was he making "debating
points?" Or did he himself actually believe such arguments?

This entire passage is one of the most closely—and

speciously—argued in the *Manifesto*. Its emotional tone is enhanced by many rhetorical devices, perhaps the most characteristic being what might be called *proportionalism*. Marx's mathematical bias and his sense of historical inevitability doubtless influenced his use of this device. Thus, he observes that "in proportion" as personal exploitation diminishes, so national exploitation will diminish. Marx uses this device often enough thoughout the work. The device is symbolized in the statement: "x is related to y as y is related to z" $(xRy:yRz)$. Other instances of this device can be found in ¶ 29, ¶ 38, ¶ 182.

But apart from stylistic characteristics there is another element of interest in this passage, and that is the equation between *personal, class*, and *national antagonisms*. Let us recall that the initial principle of the *Manifesto* is that class antagonisms characterize the whole of history. So it would follow that every personal antagonism is based on class antagonism. But how shall we explain class antagonisms incorporated in national antagonisms? Would not members of an ascendant class in one nation naturally unite with an ascendant class in another? Would not nationalism be *impossible* because of the "international bourgeois conspiracy"? Marx has tried to hint at this, but the facts of international politics run counter to his argument.

It seems unusual in a Europe so often fluttered by the ardent spirit of nationalism that Marx could so lightly have dismissed national aspirations. Was he so blinded by the "international bourgeois conspiracy" as to minimize the psychological bias of national consciousness? Or was it merely that he envisioned—like St. Paul awaiting the second coming of Christ—the proletarian revolution to be imminent? (Surely the comparison between Marx and St. Paul—however inaccurate—is at least suggestive.) Only his rhetoric seems to support the thesis that personal antagonisms are the atomic particles of class antagonism, and these in turn are the molecular units of national antagonisms.

But the communist position must be further clarified against criticism, and to this Marx eagerly turns.

s u m m a r y :   ¶ 110-120

Bourgeois accusations of a religious, philosophical, or ideological nature are easily rebutted.

c o m m e n t a r y

Marx concentrates into a single indictment three theoretical charges which his critics would likely bring forward. Since he has already suggested the arguments to rebut such charges, this passage contains a good deal of material previously used. Its distinguishing feature, however, is that it clearly dismisses all religious, philosophical, and ideological criticism framed in the categories of bourgeois conceptualization.

The rebuttal is rather simple, mostly because he has used it several times before. As Marx puts it, the conditions of human conception alter with the conditions of man's material existence. Hence, at any one moment in history, what man thinks about, contemplates, elects to sanction or revere depends entirely upon the social relations available to him. These social relations are a function of material conditions. Consequently, human conceptualization is a function of such conditions. It follows also that any criticism of a religious, philosophical, or general "ideological" nature simply betrays the bourgeois material conditions created by a bourgeois society. How could such criticism be framed from an *unbiased* viewpoint then? Do not all ruling ideas come from ruling classes?

Here again is an echo of ¶ 1: "The history of all hitherto existing society is the history of class struggle". Indeed echoes of that principle have repeatedly appeared (for example, ¶ 39 and ¶ 52).

Marx appeals to the *history of ideas* to prove his case. Such history shows that ideas change in proportion as the conditions of material production are changed. He hammers away at the same theme: "The ruling ideas of every age have always been the ideas of the ruling class" *(Die herrschenden Ideen einer Zeit waren stets nur die Ideen der heerschenden Klasse).*

When *ideas* revolutionize a society, then that society is merely expressing the implicit elements of a new society. Ancient ideas gave way to Christian ideas, just as Christian ideas gave way to Enlightenment ideas. Thus, the concept of *religious liberty* gave speech to the bourgeois concept of *free competition*. Should we assume that religion, philosophy, and the ideas of law or justice remain true no matter what society they spring from? To do so would be to trample upon the truths of history. Does it then mean that communism wishes to abolish all religion, all freedom and justice, all truths? On the contrary, says Marx, communism wishes only to expose the *class bias* of such ideas as they now stand.

Marx has come full circle in reintroducing the principle with which the *Manifesto* began. That principle in different words resounds throughout this section: "The history of all past society has consisted in the development of class antagonisms that assumed different forms at different epochs" *(Die Geschichte der ganzen bisherigen Gesellschaft bewegte sich in Klassengegensätzen, die in*

den verschiedenen Epochen verschieden gestaltet waren).
Admitttedly, the original statement of the principle is
more succinct—"The history of all hitherto existing society
is the history of class warfare" *(Die Geschichte aller bisherigen Gesellschaft ist die Geschichte von Klassenkämp-
fen).* But the sentiment expressed is a reflection of its
cardinal principle.

One point, however, is indelibly underscored, and that
is that, historically, one part of society has always exploited another. This simply suggests that all history is
essentially *homogeneous.* Its essential theme is that of
actual or symbolic exploitation. This being so, how can
anyone—communists included—alter this essential homo-
geneity? Marx ignores the issue, and substitutes the notion that because the impending communist revolution
involves the most radical disruption of traditional property relations, it must likewise involve the most radical
disruption of ruling-class ideas. Shall exploitation simply
dissolve once there are no ruling classes? Then what shall
happen to the "essence of history"? As though anticipating
such questions from his critics, Marx concludes his
treatment of criticisms against communist ideas. "But
enough of bourgeois objection to communist ideas," he
observes *(Doch lassen wir die Einwürfe der Bourgeoisie
gegen den Kommunismus).*

This portion of the *Manifesto* has been largely concerned with answering objections to communism. Now
Marx turns to more positive assertions as he concludes
Section III. His central message will be that the communist revolution will establish the proletariat as the
ruling class, and once this is done the concept of a
ruling class will vanish.

SUMMARY: ¶ 121-125

The communist revolution will begin by establishing the proletariat as the ruling class, by nationalizing all property, and by introducing basic reforms in industry, agriculture, and education.

COMMENTARY

The idea that the first stage in revolutionizing society is to be the forcible overthrow of the bourgeoisie and the elevation of the proletariat has already appeared several times before. The working class revolution can come to nothing without establishing the proletariat as the "ruling class" (*zur herrschenden Klasse*). For Marx, this is equivalent to establishing *democracy*, since *democracy* literally means "rule by the people" and only proletarians count as *people*.

The original German text rings with high revolutionary zeal, and its words might best be translated as "winning through battle the fight for democracy" (*die Erkämpfung der Democratie*). Thus the phrase "the battle for democracy" always denotes for Marx the expected insurrection of the proletariat. Marx never used the term *democracy* in any other sense.

Curiously, the idea that *establishing democracy* is equivalent to establishing "proletarian democracy" comes later in Marx's writings, and is usually associated with the well-known phrase "dictatorship of the proletariat" which Marx coined after the February, 1848, revolution in Paris, and used several times after the June insurrection. The phrase is used in 1850 in the work *The Class Wars in France (Die Klassenkämpfe in Frankreich)*, and again in the *Critique of the Gotha Program* of 1875 published by Engels in the *Neue Zeit* eight years after Marx's death. The phrase attained great prominence, however, in the writings of Lenin and Stalin, even though it does not have a commanding position in Marx's vocabulary.

Instituting *democracy* means fighting for proletarian political supremacy. But what will the proletariat do once it has gained political supremacy? It will wring from the bourgeoisie its capital advantages, and will then turn over to the control of the state *(in den Händen des Staats)* the instruments of production. Naturally, by the term *state* Marx does not mean the bureaucratic establishment created by the bourgeoisie. He means the "organized ruling proletariat." Naturally, too, the organizers of the proletariat will be the communists. Marx insists that this new form of the state will increase the total productive forces of society as rapidly as possible.

Marx admits that at first the proletarian take-over must be done despotically (thus the later phrase "dictator-ship of the proletariat") by aggrandizing the property and productive rights of the bourgeoisie. He also admits that these steps may be insufficient in insuring the success of the revolution. In different countries the exact measures to be taken will vary, but the essential purpose and design of the revolutionary method will not.

Marx then proposes ten specific measures for the most forward-looking and highly developed countries *(die fortgeschrittensten Länder)*. Today, these proposals may seem commonplace. In Marx's day they were less so but hardly novel, since others had expressed similar ideas. Together, however, these measures appeared to give *backbone* to the communist program by suggesting con-crete reforms which liberal, democratic, and revolutionary groups might all find acceptable.

Heading the list of measures is a call for the abolition

of land property. All land rents would be diverted to funding public programs for the improvement of social conditions.

Curiously, whenever Marx has used the term *property* he has meant "bourgois property," and this implied *capital* and control of the "modes of production." Here, however, Marx expressly refers to "land property" *(Grundeigentum)*. He adds that all land rents or ground-rents *(Grundrente)* should be used for public services. Then it is not particularly the bourgeoisie to whom he refers in this demand, but rather the landed aristocracy, and only incidentally those members of the bourgeoisie who own large estates. The point to notice is that once again Marx singles out a special social group—those who collect ground-rents—that is neither bourgeois nor proletarian. He ignored the existence of the landed aristocracy at first, and simplified the social antagonism between two rather than three classes (see page 51). Now he is forced to admit the importance of that third class.

Another demand which also seems aimed at the landed aristocracy (although it equally affects the bourgeoisie) is the demand to abolish all rights of inheritance. In addition, when Marx calls for the universalization of work and the equalization of the obligation of all to work *(Gleicher Arbeitszwang für alle)*, he appears to direct his remarks not merely in favor of those who can find no work but against those whom he has hitherto condemned as the class of *idle rich*. Yet, in the second demand for a "graduated income tax" he seems to assume that a class which can pay such a tax will remain in existence.

One other point about this phrase "graduated income tax." In the original German, it literally reads "Severe progressive control" *(Starke Progressivsteuer)*. The word *steuer* means *rudder* or *helm,* and by analogy would mean *control.* Coupled with the adjective *severe (starke),* the phrase seems to leave little doubt that Marx intends to tax out of existence anyone with sufficient funds to be entitled to a station above that of workers. Yet who then would be taxed?

Marx adds to this list a measure for the confiscation of property owned by emigrants and rebels *(Konfiskation des Eigentums aller Emigranten und Rebellen).* This is clearly addressed to those bourgeois property owners who would seek to flee the revolution, and those who would attempt to take arms against the revolution (and hence be "rebels"). Both would *legally* be deprived of their holdings. Hence, whatever personal property could not be extracted by heavy taxation and the abrogation of inheritance rights, or what could not be taken peacefully, would be taken *forcibly.*

The *state,* which to Marx would naturally mean the *proletarian state,* would also be empowered to centralize credit in a state bank. The *state* (that is, the proletariat) would assume control of communications, transportation, and all other industry. It would improve and bring under cultivation all wastelands, and unify agriculture and industry. Would this not, Marx perhaps thought, eradicate the distinction between towns and countryside?

Finally, the list concludes with demands for free public education, the abolition of child factory-labor, and the introduction of industrial training for workers.

All in all, the list of demands is not a formidable one. In terms of what many of Marx's contemporaries were seeking, certain items on the list had already been suggested by various groups. Its significance is that it provides the communists with what appears to be a well thought-out program of action which hinges on the abolition of private property.

S U M M A R Y : ¶ 126-127

Once the proletariat is the ruling class, the notion of a ruling class will collapse. In place of classes and class distinctions, the proletariat will substitute the free association of all peoples.

C O M M E N T A R Y

Marx's argument, tinged with dialectical logic seems simple enough.

With the nationalization of production, he reasons, class distinctions will necessarily disappear, and political power will lose its purely private character. Political power, hitherto based on class distinctions, will, with the disappearance of those distinctions, become *public* power. It will no longer be used by one man against another in the interests of class rule. Once the proletariat destroys the bourgeoisie and becomes the *ruling class*, it will necessarily sweep away all classes, and therefore all class antagonisms. With this act of self-dissolution it will have abolished its own supremacy as a class.

Marx's argument here echoes the contrapuntal play on thesis (bourgeoisie) against antithesis (proletariat) which will result in the synthesis of a *classless* society. In this case, however, the final synthesis is deprived of becoming a new thesis in a new dialectical movement. It is as though the logic of history shall have drawn to a close.

What shall take the place of ruling classes? A free association of peoples, says Marx. He can therefore conclude this section of the *Manifesto* — which has contained so many ominous statements — on an idyllic note. This "association" will be the condition in which "the free development of each is a condition for the free development of all" (*die freie Entwicklung eines jeden die Be-*

dingung für die freie Entwicklung aller ist).

This statement has, perhaps deservedly, become one of the most famous Marx ever wrote. It reveals some of the idealist tendencies that characterize his early writings. Can it, however, be squared with many of the rather hardbitten, tough-nosed statements which this revolutionary tract contains? Each reader will have to decide this for himself.

There can be no doubt, however, that this ringing formula expresses the principle of *equality* which is inherent in the tradition of British liberalism as well as of French social-democratic thought. That this principle is so clearly espoused by the communists implies that they are in the same traditions which seek the liberalization of man.

Whether or not Marx was using this sort of language as a mere political gambit (this does not seem entirely likely) or as an expression of his innermost feelings (this seems more likely) has never been settled to the satisfaction of all critics. But if this statement is linked with a statement previously made that "all we want to do away with is the miserable character of this appropriation by which the worker lives merely to increase capital," the sentiment expressed here is a plausible version of Marx's basic humanist convictions.

"Free association" of all and "free development" of all were expressions for Marx which were equivalent to the creation of a *new kind of man,* a new humanity (*neue Menscheit*), which was a constant theme of his early works. As he repeatedly said from 1843 onward, this ideal could be realized only by the most ruthless criticism of the existing order of things (*rucksichtslose Kritik alles Bestehenden*). So far, the *Manifesto* has provided this "Kritik" — done so perhaps repetitively and scornfully, but done so nonetheless.

The rest of what Marx has to say in the remaining two sections of the *Manifesto* will by comparison seem like footnotes to the first two sections. He will attempt first to compare communism with all other forms of socialism in order to show that it alone can claim the title to theoretical and practical superiority. He will then conclude with a final summation of communist views.

Section III: *Socialism and Communist Literature*

GENERAL SUMMARY: ¶ 128-184

Socialist tracts which have appeared in many quarters require careful scrutiny.

COMMENTARY

The following section, which comprises less than 30% of the *Manifesto,* considers and criticizes three main types of socialist views. Doubtless the main reason Marx includes mention of such literature is to enhance the communist position by revealing the weaknesses of its competitors.

In order to follow Marx's ideas more closely, we shall consider in greater detail each of the three main types of competitive socialism. The first of these he calls *"Reactionary Socialism;* the second, *Bourgeois Socialism;* and the third, *Critical-Utopian Socialism.*

SUMMARY: ¶ 128-138

1] **Reactionary Socialism**

a. **Feudal Socialism**

Feudal socialism is merely another form of class ex-

ploitation, and uses the common people to help defeat
feudalism's enemies.

First, Marx considers socialist theories he believes to
be polluted by class prejudice. As such, they are essentially exploitive, and are grouped under the title *Reactionary Socialism.* This type of socialism he further divides into three sub-types: *Feudal Socialism, Petty
Bourgeois Socialism,* and *German Socialism.*

Feudal socialism is born out of the desire of many
French and English aristocrats to write anti-bourgeois
literature. Surely they of all people had most to gain in
doing so. Wishing to arouse sympathy for their own position, they consequently indicted the bourgeoisie in the
name of the workers. The old aristocracy could then
take its sweet revenge "by singing lampoons against its
new master, whispering in his ears sinister prophecies of
coming catastrophe."

This then is the origin of *feudal socialism.* What was it
except "half lamentation, half lampoon, half echo of the
past, half menace of the future" (*halb Klagelied, halb
Pasquill, halb Rückhall der Vergangenheit, halb Dräuen
der Zukunft*)? Yet for all this, says Marx, it was unable
to perceive the true march of history. Aristocratic socialists have waved alm's-bags in behalf of the people. But
could anyone fail to see through such a ruse? Could anyone fail to see on their haughty backsides the old feudal
coats of arms?

As typical examples of this sort of socialism, Marx singles out the French *Legitimatists* who supported the Bourbon claims to the French throne after 1815 against the

Orleanist supporters of Louis Philippe, who was eventually crowned the *bourgeois king*. He also cites the movement known as "Young England" which included Benjamin Disraeli and other conservatives who attacked bourgeois industrialists in the interests of urban workers and peasants.

But, he argues, these antiquated aristocrats forget that they themselves were once exploiters, and gave birth to the bourgeoisie which they now seek to destroy. They are merely reactionaries who accuse the bourgeoisie of developing a class — the proletariat — that will bring down the older order. What really angers them is not so much the creation of a proletariat, as the fact that it is a *revolutionary* proletariat.

In referring to the *creation* of the proletariat, Marx has returned to a theme mentioned on several previous occasions (see ¶ 27-29, ¶ 40, and ¶ 53). He once again observes that the proletariat emerged as a direct result of the rise of the bourgeoisie only because that class exercised its exploitive instincts.

Despite high-minded phrases, says Marx, feudal reactionaries take every possible opportunity to coerce the workers, and fraternize with representatives of clerical socialism. The reference to *clerical socialism* was meant as a direct attack on the French priest Hugues de Lamennais, but it was also aimed against the general alliance between the British squirarchy and the British parsonage system. This so-called "Christian socialism," he says, is merely the "holywater with which the priest blesses the anger of the aristocrats" (*das Weihwasser, womit der Pfaffe den Ärger des Aristokraten einsegnet*). For Marx, such socialism was simply another piece of evidence demonstrating the ways in which institutional religion had hoodwinked the masses.

Although so far Marx has not made any direct attack on religion and the churches he comes closest to it here in his criticism of *clerical socialism*, and it may therefore prove useful to consider some of his ideas of the meaning of religion in human society.

Perhaps his best known condemnation of religion is found in an early work, *Critique of the Hegelian Philosophy of Law:* "Religion is the opiate of the masses." What Marx meant by this, however, and how it fits together with his sense of social reform is often obscured.

Marx was a critic of institutional religion simply because he was a critic of the society in which he lived and in which institutionalized religion held an important *ruling* position. But this is not the same as saying that he was *irreligious*, that he did not believe in the *sacred*. Man was sacred, as was the meaning of history and human experience. In order to understand this, it is necessary to review some of his statements about religion.

To begin with, Marx understood all religions as creations of culture, as cultural phenomena. Many theologians, sociologists, and anthropologists of the present day would concur in this view. In the *Critique of the Hegelian Philosophy of Law* he tried to emphasize this fact: "Man makes religion, religion does not make man."

But there is another element, one which finds its roots in the ideas of Ludwig Feuerbach. Feuerbach had reasoned that the *idea of God* is merely a reflection of the idea of man; in projecting his own best human qualities, man "creates" the idea of God. Marx accepted this basic premise as applicable to religion, and conceded in the *Critique* that "religion is the self-consciousness and self-feeling of man."

But he went further in perceiving that religion itself is

a useful *key* to understand the inner workings of a society. Man exists in a society, and what he does in that society under the sanction of religion reveals a good deal about the character of the society itself: "Religion is the general theory of that [social] world, its logic in a popular form."

In Volume I of *Capital* he would make use of the same insight by noting that "The religious world is merely the reflection of the real world." He used the same occasion to expose Christianity by saying, "And for a society based upon the production of commodities, . . . Christianity with its *cultus* of abstract man, more especially in its bourgeois developments . . . is the most fitting form of religion."

In the *Critique*, however, he tried to show that the "humanistic" struggle against institutional religion is "the fight against the other world of which religion is the spiritual aroma." The distress which is to be found in religion is therefore of great significance. It is symptomatic of something more than illusory distress; indeed it is the expression of *real* distress — "the sigh of the oppressed creature, the heart of a heartless world, just as it is the spirit of an unspiritual situation."

Because institutional religion has turned away from curing the ills of man's present experience, and has promised an easy escape to another world, it has opposed the *human* interests of man. Man's task in this world is not to speak about it like the philosophers (as he suggested in his *Theses on Feuerbach*) "but to *change* it." Religion does not want to change the world, but only to perpetuate worldly perfidies.

Hence, to unmask religion as an alienating force is to unmask the society which supports it. Thus, "the criticism of heaven turns into the criticism of the earth, the criticism of religion into the criticism of law, and the criticism of theology into the criticism of politics."

Marx's chief criticisms against religion can be summed up in three propositions: 1. religion teaches the bourgeois exploiters that they have *rights* over the poor, and at the same time 2. it teaches that the poor have a *duty* to be content with being exploited; and finally 3. religion sanctions man's passivity, and does not encourage him to change his economic conditions.

Neither Marx nor Engels was insensitive to the fact that religion had once served the purpose of giving people comfort against the hardships of existence. But in a technological world, where nature can be conquered, such comfort is anachronous.

Marx was also aware of the great differences between the pretensions, and the actuality, of Christian teaching. The social principles of Christianity, he once wrote in an article, justified the slavery of antiquity, the serfdom of the middle ages, and now sanctions the oppression of the proletariat. He concludes, "The social principles of Christianity are cringing, but the proletariat is revolutionary."

It is sometimes said that Marx was an *atheist,* and that this accounts for his opposition to the churches as social insitutions. To support his "atheism," his critics quote his doctoral dissertation, *On the Difference Between the Natural Philosophy of Democritus and Epicurus,* which evidences Marx's preference for Epicurean materialism as "an energizing principle." And he is credited with the saying: "In one word, I hate all gods."

But it is probably more accurate to say that Marx was an *anti-theist,* whose position was an essentially *religious* reaction, not against religion as such, but against religious institutions which had condoned and even defended "religious" exploitation. Much has been written about the religious intuitions of Marx and even Marxism — at least enough to warn the student that this is a complicated topic.

For example, is "Marxism" a competitive religion? Economist Joseph Schumpeter once said: Definitely. Marxism is a religion which provides a system of ultimate explanations of all human experience and a plan of salvation for mankind.

Recent talks between Marxists and Christians, particularly in France, have shown each the possibilities of religious insight in "Marxism." Roger Garaudy, a French Marxist, has been significantly engaged in such talks.

But after this excursion on Marx's views on religion we must return to the main outlines of his criticism of competitive brands of socialism.

SUMMARY: ¶ 139-145

b. Petty Bourgeois Socialism

This is another reactionary form of socialism which has its roots in the old burgher-peasant society.

COMMENTARY

German and French society constitute the main target of Marx's criticism in this section where he argues against those who are no less misguided than feudal reactionaries.

He admits that medieval burghers and peasant proprietors were precursors of the modern industrial bourgeoisie. In non-industrial countries, he caustically observes, the remnants of these groups have vegetated side by side with the rising industrial bourgeoisie. In countries where industrialization has taken place, however, this same petty bourgeoisie is gradually sinking into the proletariat. But to forestall doing so, it identifies itself with the reactionary views of its progenitors.

One example of this kind of petty bourgeois sentiment Marx finds in the work of Jean Charles Sismondi, a Swiss historian-economist. Sismondi, who influenced Marx in many ways, opposed the bourgeois doctrine of *laissez-faire* (or free-trade) economics.

As Sismondi is Marx's German target, so Proudhon is his French target. In France, where half the population belongs to the peasant class anyway, says Marx, it was easy (he means for such people as Proudhon) to side with the proletarians against bourgeois oppression. There it was also easy to expose the hypocrisy of *laissez-faire* economic theory (as Proudhon had done), and to cry out against the misery of the proletarians.

Marx does not hesitate, however, to assert that such criticism as Sismondi or Proudhon mounted "is both reactionary and utopian" (*ist er reaktionär und utopistisch zugleich*). Stubborn facts, Marx argues, continue to reveal the deceptions of this group — why else, for example would its members support the guild system and patriarchial agriculture? Such "socialism" merely tries to turn back the clock.

SUMMARY: ¶ 146-162

c.   German or "True" Socialism

German socialism is equally reactionary. It turned French ideas into philosophical fantasy, and became the dupe of monarchist governments and petty bourgeois philistinism.

COMMENTARY

Finally, Marx verbally scorns the "obfuscating" German literature which at one time influenced his own ideas. His main target is the heritage of "German idealism" and its misguided attempt to express French social-democratic ideas. This is all the more interesting since German idealism and French social democracy provided two of the essential ingredients of his own views. (See pages 27ff.)

When the German bourgeoisie began to dismantle the social and political supremacy of feudalism, they employed French socialist ideas to do so. Marx's own father, for example, was a disciple of Voltaire and Rousseau, and rather representative of this view.

The major error made by Germans when they accepted these ideas was to assume that the social conditions reflected in such French literature was duplicated in Germany. To German philosophers enamoured of Kant's philosophy of *"practical reason"* — the kind of reason capable of dealing with moral problems — the French Revolution was largely a *moral* issue. Thus, into German philosophical tradition there was gradually poured strong doses of French socialist literature, but the resulting mixture was oil and water.

But the objection may arise: "If Marx criticizes the mixture of German idealistic philosophy and French social-democratic ideas, how could *he* have combined both traditions, and done it so successfully?"

The answer is difficult to state simply and at the same time accurately. But two points may be made. (1) While Marx admitted his debt on separate occasions to German idealist thinkers — for example, Fichte and Hegel — and to French socialist theorists — for instance, Babeuf, Buonarotti, and Saint-Simon — he never admitted *combining* them in the way that he is here criticizing. (2) Moreover,

Marx would never admit — this was one of his most characteristic traits — that he had the "wrong ideas" about anything.

The objection, however well put, still misses the point that Marx is trying to make here. It is not so much the *combination* of these traditions as the *wrong* combination that he is criticizing. He is particularly annoyed with those who could not distinguish between the developmental stages reached by the more industrialized France and the less industrialized Germany.

In attempting to suggest the stupidity of combining these traditions, Marx reminds his readers of the practice of medieval monks who penned their own works on top of classical manuscripts. What the Germans did was to mimic this process by writing French social criticism in the language of abstract German philosophy. Empty phrases, drawn largely from a Hegelian vocabulary, were used to describe French criticism of its own political and economic processes. Instead of writing about the economic functions of money, German writers would babble about the "alienation of humanity." For the French criticism of the bourgeois state, Germans would write about the "dethronement of the category of the general."

Since Marx had been nourished on such literature, his indignation runs high. Germans, he says, had the nerve to call this "true socialism" when all they had done was to emasculate French social theory. They aimed such foolishness not at the proletarians, but at some *abstract imitation man* "who belongs to no class, above all to no reality, but only to the vaporous heaven of some philosophical fantasy" (*der keine Klasse, der überhaupt nich der Wirklichkeit, der nur dem Dunsthimmel der philosophischen Phantasie angehört*). Why, Marx asks, has such schoolboy "socialism" been taken so seriously?

Because, he answers, it served the interests of reactionary groups. Why should Germans so vehemently oppose representative government, freedom of the press, liberty and equality? Because all these were mistaken for attempts at bourgeois aggrandisement. How welcome to German squires, parsons, and professors, he observes, were such reactionary views. How excellent an antidote against bourgeois threats was "true socialist" prose. For such people and for representatives of absolutist German governments — just then completing their own flogging of the German working class — what better brand of socialism could one imagine?

With telling effect Marx then explains that this "true socialism" merely served the interests of monarchic governments against the bourgeoisie. And not only was it a weapon against the German bourgeoisie, it was also a stick to beat the German working classes. But behind such "socialism" there always lurked German philistines who are fundamentally reactionary. On the surface, there is a great deal of noise about German socialism, but underneath lies the German petty bourgeoisie, a relic of the sixteenth century. What better way, Marx argues, to preserve the *status quo* than to preserve this class? the real enemies of this "true socialism" are the industrial bourgeoisie and the revolutionary proletariat.

Marx saves some of his bitterest language to describe the theoreticians of German socialism. They have, he says, wrapped their eternal truths in the raiment "of speculative spiderweb, embroidered it with the esthete's oratorical flowers, soaked it through with the oppressive sentimentality of an emotional backwater" (*aus spekulativem Spinnweb, überstickt mit schöngeistigen Redeblumen, durchtränkt von liebesschwülem Gemütstau*). They had no difficulty in selling their contemporaries a bill of

goods. But behind the bombastic rhetoric of German socialism was the sly petty bourgeois philistine — the model
of his nation, after whom his nation patterned itself. His
every hidden meanness could be extolled as a lofty ideal.
And all these "ideals" together have so often attempted
to crush communism and communist publications.

The shrill, emotional quality of this passage is, of course,
squeezed out of Marx's personal experiences as an editor
of "communist" publications. He himself had known what
it meant to be hunted from one city to another by Prussian
governmental officials.

SUMMARY: ¶ 163-170

2]   Conservative or Bourgeois Socialism

**Some members of the bourgeoisie espouse socialist doc-
trines — despite the patent contradictions — in order to
safeguard their own position.**

COMMENTARY

Marx seems to take particular delight in exposing the
pretensions of some members of the bourgeois class who
wish to reform social grievances. Why should they do so
except out of a pure desire to survive? Economists, humanitarians, temperance fanatics — all of them are motivated by the sheer will to secure the continued existence of the bourgeoisie. If Marx had known the expression, he might have characterized this group by the slogan: "If you can't beat them, join them."

What bothered him most, though, were the pretensions
of such reactionary "socialists" to systematise their doctrines in great detail. Here Marx makes special mention

of Pierre Proudhon's book *The Philosophy of Poverty* as an example of exotic systematization. When this book was first published in 1846, it provided Marx the opportunity the following year of issuing a rejoinder, which he entitled *The Poverty of Philosophy* (*Misère de la philosophie*). Proudhon's book — the full title of which was *The System of Economic Paradoxes, or the Philosophy of Poverty* (*Système des contradictions économiques ou philosophie de la misère*) — sought to combine philosophy, social and economic theory, and political science in a way that Marx himself would later imitate with greater success.

Proudhon said that capitalism perpetuated inequality, which the French Revolution had promised to destroy. But he himself had little genuine understanding of the workings of capitalism. Marx's answer left little doubt that the Proudhonian motto, "Property is theft," was in his eyes another of Proudhon's empty phrases.

In addition to all systematic forms of bourgeois socialism, Marx asserts, there is another, more practical form which preaches against revolutionary change. Instead, it seeks to bring about changes through administrative procedures. It therefore tries to redeem the excesses of beourgeois social and economic practice through *reform* rather than *revolution*. But what, Marx coldly points out, would such a solution produce except the enhancement of bourgeois governmental power?

Marx concludes that "bourgeois socialism" is a mere figure of speech. What do the phrases *free trade, protective duties, prison reform* mean? For the benefit of the working class? Not on your life. We might almost say that "the bourgeois are bourgeois — for the benefit of the working class" (*die Bourgeois Bourgeois sind — im Interesse der arbeitenden Klasse*).

And with that flourish Marx dismisses the case against "bourgeois socialism."

SUMMARY: ¶ 171-184

3]   Critical-Utopian Socialism

Some other forms of socialism lack historical perspective and theoretical acumen, and are motivated by sheer sentimentality.

COMMENTARY

Marx introduces his remarks on *critical-utopian* social-ism by absolving from criticism all those *revolutionary* writers who have ever voiced the interests of the prole-tariat. He particularly singles out François Babeuf, a revolutionary leader who was executed during the French Terror for preaching economic and political equality.

He then admits that all previous attempts to establish the supremacy of the proletariat naturally failed because the proper economic conditions were absent. In the next place, revolutionary literature which accompanied the emergence of the proletariat was fundamentally reaction-ary in intent. It called for asceticism and a crude sort of social levelling, and was consequently ineffective.

Marx then considers several utopion-socialist doctrines. First to be mentioned are the ideas of Saint-Simon, who had exerted great influence on Auguste Comte. Saint-Simon had proposed the reorganization of society into scientifically supervised groups. He believed that such re-organization would eventually develop better living and working conditions for the great masses of the poor. Then there were François Fourier in France and Robert Owen in England who advocated and actually set up commune settlements of workers. These groups, Marx asserts, grew up in the early and undeveloped period of the struggle between the bourgeoisie and the proletariat. Men such as Fourier and Owen were aware of the *fact* of class antagonism. What they were ignorant of was the historical *meaning* of the class struggle.

Class antagonisms, Marx argues, are proportional to the industrial development of a society. But the Saint-Simon-Owen-Fourier types have been blind to the fact that there are *material conditions* which anticipate and prepare the way for the emancipation of the proletariat. They have spent their time in looking for extraneous *laws of society* to account for social conditions. Instead of investing in historical action, they have invented personal fantasies. They confuse the proletariat with *those who suffer most.* And believing themselves to be above the heat and dust of class conflicts, they envision the social improvement of all classes. Naturally, such views make an appealing curtsy to the ruling class. These men only enhance this appeal because they reject revolutionary action, and seek strictly peaceful means to spread their social gospel.

Marx, however, is less harsh on advocates of this brand of socialism. So far as the development of society is concerned, he says, such doctrines are theoretically at a very early stage, a stage which coincides with only the most primitive urgings of society searching for renewal and redemption. Still, socialist writings of this type contain many useful criticisms of existing society, and therefore can be of particular use to the working classes. When such socialists call for elimination of the distinction between town and country, or the abolition of the family, private gain, and the wage system, they are utopian in

every sense. Their real significance is that they have revealed the hidden springs of historical development,
which they have nonetheless studiously ignored.

In proportion as the struggle between bourgeois and
proletarian classes takes place, Marx reasons, utopian fantasies lose all practical and theoretical justification. As
they dream of *home workshops,* vest-pocket redemption,
or *castles in the air* — Marx is thinking of the communes
founded by Fourier and Cabet — they appeal to bourgeois purse strings and to bourgeois sentiment. Consequently, they are both reactionary and anti-revolutionary.
Whenever utopians undertake political action they oppose
the working class. Owenites opposed *Chartism.* Fourierists opposed *Reformism.* Both movements, however ill-
conceived, tried to bring about some kind of political
difference in their societies. Chartism, Marx's readers
would know, had been active from 1837 as a political
movement to obtain the right to vote for all males of legal
age, whether or not they were property owners, and also
sought to enforce voting by secret ballot. Reformism —
named after the *Réformistes* who published the Paris
newspaper *La Réforme* — was a republican revolutionary
movement.

Marx has now concluded his consideration of competitive forms of socialistic doctrines in order to demonstrate
their weaknesses in comparison with the strengths, both
practical and theoretic, of the communists.

In the preceding two sections, he has shown the relations of the communists to other working-class parties
(Section II) and to the general literature of socialist
movements (Section III). Now he can turn his attention
to the relationship between communists and politically
entrenched "opposition parties."

Section IV: *Position of Communists in Relation to Various Opposition Parties*

SUMMARY: ¶ 185-196

Communists are the most advanced of all anti-establishment parties. They seek to bring about the revolution in every European country.

COMMENTARY

Marx takes this last opportunity to restate the communist position, and to align its strategy wih existing political parties that had some kind of institutional position from which to act. It soon becomes evident that the political strategy of the communists is to remain "pliable," and to back whatever group could serve their interests.

First, Marx reiterates the communists' intention to achieve proletarian supremacy and to enforce proletarian financial interests. He emphasizes (as he did in ¶58-59) that communists not only serve the proletarian movement in the present crisis, but continue to work to insure the future success of that movement. "The revolution," as he said elsewhere, "does not simply *happen;* it must be *made.*"

Then, country by country, he reveals the political strategy of the communists. In France, communists ally themselves with the Social-Democrats as represented by Louis Blanc and the *Réformistes.* In Switzerland, they strike a cautious bargain with the radicals. In Poland, they support agrarian revolution. In Germany, they join the bourgeoisie whenever it fights in a revolutionary way against monarchy, squirearchy, and the petty bourgeoisie. Earlier in the *Critique of the Hegelian Philosophy of Law,* Marx had prophesied that "In Germany no brand of serfdom can be exterminated without extirpating every kind of serfdom."

Like a lengthy footnote to the remarks he has already made in section II, Marx hammers away at the claim that communists never cease to instill in the working classes a consciousness of the struggle in which they are engaged. In 1850, Marx would issue a *Circular of the Central Committee to the League of Communists* instructing its readers to join the *petty bourgeois democrats* against any faction which *they* aim to overthrow, but "to oppose them in everything whereby they seek to consolidate their position." It is "to our interest," Marx concludes, "to make the revolution permanent." Marx imagines, even now in the *Manifesto*, that when the reactionaries in Germany are toppled from power, then the proletarians will be able to turn against the bourgeoisie.

Germany is of particular interest to the communists, says Marx, only because it is on the brink of a bourgeois revolution against aristocratic rule. This bourgeois revolution is to Marx merely the harbinger of the ultimate proletarian revolution. Of course, events proved otherwise than Marx predicted, and Germany maintained its petty bourgeois bias, and eventually united under Otto von Bismarck.

Three telegraphic statements sum up for Marx the communist tactics:1. to support every revolutionary movement against the existing political and social orders;   2. to emphasize in every possible instance the inequity of private property;   and 3. to work for the unification of "democratic parties in all countries," by which he naturally means *workers' parties*.

With his final remarks, Marx once again employs the tone of terror which prefaced the *Manifesto*. First, he repeats the theme that concludes the *Preface*, namely, that communists no longer conceal their intentions to overthrow the existing order of things. Secondly, he follows this by sentences that both threaten and encourage: "Let the ruling classes tremble at a communist revolution. Proletarians have nothing to lose but their chains. They have a world to win." (*Mögen die herrschenden Klassen vor einer kommunistischen Revolution zittern. Die Proletarier haben nichts in ihr zu verlieren als ihre Ketten. Sie haben eine Welt zu gewinnen*).

The concluding motto in the *Manifesto* Marx had substituted for the accepted slogan of the Communist League. To this slogan — "All men are brothers" — Marx once replied that there were many men whom he did not care to recognize as brothers. In place of this slogan Marx penned what has since become a revolutionary rallying cry: "Proletarians of all countries, unite" (*Proletarier aller Länder, vereinigt euch*).

These final lines were completed a month before the February 24 insurrections in Paris. Within a short time, other European cities ignited. On March 13, fighting broke out in Vienna; two days later, the citizens of Prague marched through the streets demanding civil liberties and the abolition of serfdom. By April, a French translation of the *Manifesto* appeared in Paris, two months before the June uprisings, which, incidentally, were the only ones involving questions of workingmen's rights.

Paradoxically, the *Manifesto* of revolution had no effect whatever on any of these revolutionary events. Paradoxically, too, Marx's rejection of nationalism was contradicted by a certain nationalist bias of his own which is revealed in a 17-point program he wrote from Paris in

March, 1848, to clarify the demands of The Communist League for Germany. Heading the list is the sentence: "All Germany is declared a simple, indivisible republic." Marx, ironically, also admits that these new demands can be realized without revolution.

The 17-point program is moderate in tone, but includes some of the material from ¶121-125 of the *Manifesto*. From Barman, Engels wrote Marx during the same month: "If a single copy of our seventeen-point program were to be distributed here, then we would be finished."

However complicated and tortuous the later history of the *Manifesto*, it never fulfilled Marx's expectations or predictions. As time wore on, Western, technically advanced countries were less affected by its claims. But in Russia, it touched sensitive nerves.

Marx always resented the fact that in the West, particularly in England, he was never accorded the recognition he felt was his due. His first volume of *Capital*, for example, was not translated into English until four years after his death, but appeared in a pirated Russian edition the year after it was first published. He called it an irony of fate that "the Russians whom I have fought for twenty-five years, and not only in German but in French and English, have always been my 'patrons.'" Before he died, Marx had to admit that, while Russia was the bulwark and reserve army of counter-revolution, "revolution will begin in the East."

As a statement of principles, the *Manifesto* never lost for Marx its *essential* validity. Its detailed observations, he confessed in the "Preface" to a German re-issue of 1872, needed revision. He added, however, that "the general principles laid down in this Manifesto are, on the whole, as correct today as ever." For the new edition, Marx refused to up-date his treatment of socialist literature in section III, and admitted that while the remarks in section IV were "in principle still correct, yet in practice [they] are antiquated."

In another German edition in 1890, seven years after Marx died, Engels boasted that the *Manifesto* is "the most widely circulated . . . of all socialist literature" and "reflects the history of the modern working class movement since 1848." The boast was dramatic, if somewhat inaccurate.

But the last word on the *Manifesto* belongs to Marx himself: In the 1872 "Preface" he perceived that "the Manifesto has become a historical document which we no longer have any right to alter."

He was right.

6

Some Critical Opinions

> *Critics usually either flatter or censure Karl Marx.*
> *On rare occasions, he is criticized with judicious*
> *balance. The extent of comment on Marx and*
> *his works is considerable, and no attempt can be*
> *made here to do more than suggest examples of*
> *Western comments — some favorable, some un-*
> *favorable, and some "judicious." In addition to*
> *selected titles cited at the end of this book,*
> *students may also want to consult* Marxist
> Philosophy: A Bibliographical Guide *by John*
> *Lachs* (*Chapel Hill, University of North*
> *Carolina,* 1967).

Erich Fromm

Fromm ranks among the most sympathetic of Marx's Western commentators. A psychoanalyst who leans heavily in his interpretations on the early manuscripts Marx wrote before 1844, Fromm deplores the distortion which Marx's ideas have suffered at the hands of English-speaking peoples.

In his *Marx's Concept of Man,* Fromm singles out *materialism* as Marx's most abused *idea.* Marx's *materialism* is usually interpreted to mean that the *profit motive* is man's dominant motivation. Fromm denies the validity of this interpretation, and argues that, on the contrary, Marx wished to free men from the chains of economic determinism, to enable them to find unity and harmony in experience.

Marx's materialism really refers to the philosophical view that matter in motion is the fundamental constituent of the universe. This was Marx's central notion. What he fought against were 1. materialism in the bourgeois sense, and 2. abstract materialism which had invaded nineteenth-century natural science. Marx never used the phrases *historical materialism* or *dialectical materialism.* His essential philosophical position was *naturalism or humanism,* which is a synthesis of *idealism* and *materialism.*

Fromm believes that Marx, in attempting to free men from the pressures of economic needs, was helping them relate more fully to humanity and to Nature. Hence, in Fromm's vocabulary, two themes play fundamental roles. These are "psychological alienation" and *ideology.*

"Alienation" implies man's inner dismemberment and estrangement from other men and the world. Secondly, like Freud, Marx taught that most men think through "false consciousness," and this he called *ideology.* By *ideology* Marx meant the whole network of conceptualizations rooted in a specific social organization. When men *think,* they use *social* categories, and are unconscious of the true wellsprings of their thoughts and actions.

Fromm also takes a strong line in defending Marx against charges of personal aberration — that he was *lonely, spiteful, arrogant,* and *authoritarian.* Fromm admits that Marx's literary style is sarcastic and that he was an aggressive defender of everything he considered to be right. He hated sham and hypocrisy, and was incapable of insincerity.

Neither a fanatic nor an opportunist, Fromm asserts, Marx represented the flowering of Western humanistic ideas.

Sidney Hook

Another generally sympathetic but more complex estimate of Marx has been given by philosopher Sidney Hook. In three books, *Toward the Understanding of Karl Marx* (1933), *From Hegel to Marx* (1936), and *Marx and the Marxists* (1955), Hook details the growth of Marx's ideas.

In his first book, he went to particular pains to argue that the apparent *contradictions* in Marx's thought have a fundamentally rational explanation:

> "The apparent contradictions in Marx's thought may arise from the fact that he was forced to defend his views against various critics and thus was forced to shift emphases in his own work. While a case of flagrant self-contradiction may be made against him, when his work is taken in context and his critics' polar positions accounted for, the charge of self-contradictions is less forceful."

Hook also pays special attention to Marx's synthesis of themes inherent in Western tradition. He was, and will continue to be, one of history's most influential figures. Hook regrets that Marx became a political symbol evoking emotional rather than logical reactions, and that he is often condemned without being read. A revolutionary rather than an academician, Marx developed his ideas in response to concrete events and in an effort to influence those events.

Being a strong believer in the dignity of man and being of a Promethean temperament, says Hook, Marx could trace his heritage to Greek ideals of scientific inquiry and humanist belief in freedom, equality, and personal integrity — beliefs which *totalitarian* followers of Marx reject.

Finally, Hook argues that Marx's intellectual legacy has been rich but ambiguous. The main reason for the ambiguity is that his immediate disciples were largely drawn, not from the European working class, but from middle-class intellectuals who "popularized" and "adapted" his ideas.

Karl Federn

Among the most ascerbic of Marx's critics is Karl Federn whose book *The Materialist Conception of History* (1939) attempted to explain the *success* of Marx's "economic theory of history."

First of all, Federn says, economic theories provide easy reference frames for all kinds of facts. Secondly, Marx's system, created out of these facts, has a certain orderly and logical face on it. But this sort of order and conclusiveness, Federn adds, appeals mostly to young and less critical minds. Marx's system is basically simple, and requires no hard work or subtlety to master its general outlines.

That system, says Federn, is also essentially *dangerous* because many of its propositions are accepted as though they had the force of religious dogma.

Federn insists that Marx offered little proof of his assertions, but merely promulgated them. Every one of his major ideas is open to serious question. For instance, the idea that *economic production* is basic in society and that *cultural life* is secondary is utterly untenable. First, Federn observes, it is impossible to demonstrate the dependence of all intellectual life on the conditions of production. Thus, it is false to say that *economic conditions* determine *intellectual life.* Intellectual and other cultural phenomena are compatible with different modes of production. Furthermore, despite identical modes of production in some societies, the greatest difference can be found in their intellectual and political life. Contrary to the Marxian thesis, the *human mind plays the decisive role* in economics and production itself.

Hence the alleged division between an "intellectual super-structure" and an *economic sub-structure* is unthinkable. The human mind plays an active role in social revolution, while productive forces are always passive. No productive force can discover itself.

Federn concedes that if Marx had used a different vocabulary — for example, "man's increasing command over productive forces" rather than "development of productive forces" — he would have been more correct.

Federn matches against Marx's *dialectical* theory the events of European history, and asserts that the whole notion of *dialectical development* is *shaky.* Historical evolution does not invariably move through a series of contradictions. Comparing the principal tendencies of European history since the end of antiquity — economic, religious, artistic and intellectual, moral and ethical — Federn argues that the "evolution" in every aspect of life proceeds on one occasion by a transition from one state to its opposite (e. g., revolution and reaction), and at another time by development in a straight, unbroken line, sometimes at a rapid pace and sometimes slowly. History passes on in an endless stream. No one knows the beginning or end of a historic period. Hence, all attempts to draw lines of historical division are artificial and arbitrary.

Marx's chief fault lay, Federn concludes, in the fact that he tended to invert everything, and was always "turning things upside down."

Benedetto Croce

Born of a wealthy family whose eminence enabled him to live comfortably and to be elected a life-member of the Italian Senate, Croce spent his early university career deeply involved in the study of Marx. In 1900 he published a study of Marx which was later translated (1914) as *Historical Materialism and the Economics of Karl Marx* in which he contrasted Marx and Hegel. Marx came off second best.

What Marx did, Croce points out, was to dress Hegelianism in materialistic and economic garb. But he added nothing new in speculative or logical insights. What Marx accepted from Hegel (Croce said elsewhere) modern criticism has since rejected in Hegel.

Principally, Marx was a Utopian. And he "remained in his innermost thought, a Utopian." In his early comments, Croce called Marx "the Machiavelli of the proletariat," but later softened this criticism.

In an essay "The Historical Materialism of Marx and His Alleged Promotion of Communism from Utopia to Science," Croce contends that Marx's doctrine is without philosophical significance, and, furthermore is filled with logical errors. He admits that Marx was a notable political figure of his day, and even concedes that Marx's theory of economic materialism opened up certain valuable areas for speculation. But the claim that he raised communism from utopia to a science "is an illusion."

Croce also admits that Marx indirectly contributed to

the success of the Russian Revolution, but adds wryly that Marx would have disowned what resulted from it:

> "Possibly Karl Marx would be astounded if he could see what has taken place in Russia and elsewhere under the standard of his name and teachings; and perhaps he would be aggrieved for he doubtless dreamed, at least in his youth, of a perfect society. . . ."

That Croce had great respect for Marx personally he shows on several occasions. But, equally so, he considered him naive and more to be pitied than ridiculed:

> "Marx in the 40 years of his political life paid the price of many disillusionments for having erected in the *Communist Manifesto* the illusion of an imminent catastrophe and collapse of the bourgeoisie, and of a rapid leap from the reign of Necessity to the reign of Liberty into a more-or-less Fourieristic harmonious paradise."

Croce also admits a grudging admiration for Marx's personal qualities which he once described:

> "A believer's enthusiasm and ardor, an apostle's unshakable endurance, which made him consecrate his entire life, plagued by poverty and suffering, to the attempted realization of his dream, cannot be denied . . . to Marx."

Thus, Croce had to admit in the end that "My disdain is not inflamed against him, even if I am forced to refute his theories. . . ."

Sir Isaiah Berlin

A British historian known for his painstaking research and lively style, Berlin's study, *Karl Marx: His Life and Environment* (1939), is usually regarded as a model of balance.

Berlin admits that one who wishes to analyze the changing quality of the life of his own society must automatically employ the categories of analysis which Marx constructed.

Personally, Berlin observes, Marx lacked the qualities of popular greatness. Yet despite such defects he has had a profound effect on mankind — indeed greater than that of any other nineteenth-century thinker.

By temperament Marx was a theorist, and avoided direct contact with the masses. He was equally repulsed by the rhetoric of the intellectuals and the complacency of the bourgeoisie. He neither conceded nor invited concessions in his dealings. Above all he hated romanticism, sentimentality, and humanitarianism.

Berlin reasons that from the mass of doctrines and insights of his predecessors and contemporaries Marx drew clear answers and directives for action. These stand as his single principal achievement. The system he developed was a massive and theoretically invulnerable structure which has altered the history of human thought in such a way that after it "certain things could never again be plausibly said."

Balanced against all other qualities — good or bad — Berlin sees Marx as a man with a single objective, and a strong will dedicated to achieving it. Thus, what distinguished Marx from his contemporaries was not his dogmatism, originality, or violence, but his single-mindedness which absorbed every word and act of his life. He dedicated himself to the practical end of founding a new faith. So he looms in history as one of the great authoritarian founders of a new faith which interprets the world in terms of a single passionate principle, and at the same time denounces all attempts to confute it. Though not pathological, Berlin admits, Marx was somewhat of a fanatic in holding to this most formidable indictment against an entire social order.

Although not in general sympathy with Federn's criticism of the "Marxian inversion," Berlin admits that there is a certain paradoxical amusement in the relationship between Marx's general assessment of the role of ideas in society and the status of Marxist ideas in the twentieth century. Marx's theory attempted to show how deeply ideas are influenced by action rather than the other way around:

> "It set out to refute the proposition that ideas decisively determine the course of history, but the very extent of its own influence on human affairs has weakened the force of its thesis."

Joseph Schumpeter

A Harvard economist and historian of economics, Schumpeter is usually considered one of Marx's fairest critics and most helpful commentators. In *Capitalism, Socialism and Democracy* (1950), Schumpeter devoted several chapters to Marx's ideas, and tried to show that the growth of democratic institutions inevitably leads to their *socialization*.

Marx, Schumpeter writes, was no mere purveyor of slogans. If this were all he could lay claim to, his name would long ago have been forgotten. Fundamentally, Marx was a prophet, and he must be seen in terms of his own age, employing the techniques of economic, historical, and sociological analysis.

The slogan *class consciousness*, Schumpeter concedes, while undoubtedly a poor formulation of workingmen's psychology, ultimately ennobled it. Like every genuine prophet, Marx saw himself as merely the humble voice of his deity, founding a new religion, preaching the logic of the dialectical processes of history. But he did this with a kind of dignity that compensates for all the pettinesses in his life and work.

Schumpeter points out that what Marx was, and what he tried to do, are to be carefully distinguished from what he became in the portraits drawn by others, and from what they tried to do with his ideas. Marxists and Bolshevists, Schumpeter argues, merely canonized an idol:

> "And, it is only characteristic of such processes of canonization that there is, between the true meaning of Marx's message and bolshevist practice and ideology, at least as great a gulf as there was between the religion of humble Galileans and the practice and ideology of the princes of the church or the war lords of the Middle Ages."

As an economist and economic historian, Schumpeter tries to give a balanced picture. It is foolish, he remarks, to ask if Marx *failed* as an economist, since in economic analysis there is no such thing as unqualified success or failure. As an economist, Marx was essentially a learned man, and his arguments always went to the root of every matter, as did those of David Ricardo from whom he learned the art of economic theorizing.

Marx, Schumpeter believes, was the first economist of top rank to teach systematically how economic theory can be turned into historical analysis, and how the narrative of history becomes evidence for theories propounded about it. Moreover, his economic, historical, and sociological theories are so intertwined that it is almost impossible to distinguish them. For example, the economic category *labor* is in principle indistinguishable from the sociological category *proletariat*.

Schumpeter concedes that Marx preached "an economic interpretation of history," but adds that it was no more *materialistic* than Hegel's. Moreover, he says, this theory stands as one of the greatest achievements of Marx's day, even though it was then misinterpreted and still is. Marx never held that religions, schools of art and philosophy, ethical ideas and political policies were either reducible to economic motives or at best unimportant. Instead, he tried to unveil the economic conditions which shape them, and account for their rise and fall.

Marx's central argument is summed up in the proposition that the economic process in a democracy tends to "socialize" itself. Therefore, the technological, organizational, commercial, administrative, and psychological prerequisites of socialism tend increasingly to be fulfilled.

In his *History of Economic Analysis* (1951), Schumpeter admitted that the fascination of Marx's work remains, no matter what position one takes toward him. The assumptions, the techniques he employed are open to many serious objections, but despite this, says Schumpeter,

> ". . . the totality of his vision, as a totality, asserts its right in every detail and is precisely the source of the intellectual fascination experienced by everyone, friend as well as foe, who makes a study of him."

Three main propositions are included in Schumpeter's estimate of Marx's *vision*. First, there is the notion of an imminent evolution of the economic process working through accumulation, which tends to undermine the economy, and therefore the society based upon that economy. Secondly, there is the idea that capitalism is being destroyed by its very achievements — and, likewise, the society which provides its social structure. Thirdly, there is the conviction that these events will give birth to another type of social organization.

THE COMMUNIST MANIFESTO*

KARL MARX [AND FRIEDRICH ENGELS]

Preface

A spectre is haunting Europe — the spectre of Communism. All the Powers of old Europe have entered into a holy alliance to exorcise this spectre: Pope and Czar, Metternich and Guizot, French Radicals and German police-spies.

Where is the party in opposition that has not been decried as Communistic by its opponents in power? Where the Opposition that has not hurled back the branding reproach of Communism, against the more advanced opposition parties, as well as against its reactionary adversaries?

Two things result from this fact.

I. Communism is already acknowledged by all European Powers to be itself a Power.

II. It is high time that Communists should openly, in the face of the whole world, publish their views, their aims, their tendencies, and meet this nursery tale of the Spectre of Communism with a Manifesto of the party itself.

To this end, Communists of various nationalities have assembled in London, and sketched the following Manifesto, to be published in the English, French, German, Italian, Flemish and Danish languages.

* From the English translation edited by Frederich Engels, 1888.

I

BOURGEOIS AND PROLETARIANS

¶ 1   The history of all hitherto existing society is the history of class struggles.

¶ 2   Freeman and slave, patrician and plebeian, lord and serf, guild-master and journeyman, in a word, oppressor and oppressed, stood in constant opposition to one another, carried on an uninterrupted, now hidden, now open fight, a fight that each time ended, either in a revolutionary re-constitution of society at large, or in the common ruin of the contending classes.

¶ 3   In the earlier epochs of history, we find almost everywhere a complicated arrangement of society into various orders, a manifold gradation of social rank.   In ancient Rome we have patricians, knights, plebeians, slaves; in the Middle Ages, feudal lords, vassals, guild-masters, journeymen, apprentices, serfs; in almost all of these classes, again, subordinate gradations.

¶ 4   The modern bourgeois society that has sprouted from the ruins of feudal society has not done away with class antagonisms. It has but established new classes, new conditions of oppression, new forms of struggle in place of the old ones.

5   Our epoch, the epoch of the bourgeoisie, possesses, however, this distinctive feature: it has simplified the class antagonisms. Society as a whole is more and more splitting up into two great hostile camps, into two great classes directly facing each other: Bourgeoisie and Proletariat.

6   From the serfs of the Middle Ages sprang the chartered burghers of the earliest towns. From these burgesses the first elements of the bourgeoisie were developed.

7   The discovery of America, the rounding of the Cape, opened up fresh ground for the rising bourgeoisie. The East-Indian and Chinese markets, the colonisation of America, trade with the colonies, the increase in the means of exchange and in commodities generally, gave to commerce, to navigation, to industry, an impulse never before known, and thereby, to the revolutionary element in the tottering feudal society, a rapid development.

8   The feudal system of industry, under which industrial production was monopolised by closed guilds, now no longer sufficed for the growing wants of the new markets. The manufacturing system took its place. The guild-masters were pushed on one side by the manufacturing middle class; division of labour between the different corporate guilds vanished in the face of division of labour in each single workshop.

9   Meantime the markets kept ever growing, the demand ever rising. Even manufacture no longer sufficed. Thereupon, steam and machinery revolutionized industrial production. The place of manufacture was taken by the giant, Modern Industry, the place of the industrial middle class, by industrial

millionaires, the leaders of whole industrial armies, the modern bourgeois.

10   Modern industry has established the world market, for which the discovery of America paved the way. This market has given an immense development to commerce, to navigation, to communication by land. This development has, in its turn, reacted on the extension of industry; and in proportion as industry, commerce, navigation, railways extended, in the same proportion the bourgeoisie developed, increased its capital, and pushed into the background every class handed down from the Middle Ages.

11   We see, therefore, how the modern bourgeoisie is itself the product of a long course of development, of a series of revolutions in the modes of production and of exchange.

12   Each step in the development of the bourgeoisie was accompanied by a corresponding political advance of that class. An oppressed class under the sway of the feudal nobility, an armed and self-governing association in the mediaeval commune; here independent urban republic (as in Italy and Germany), there taxable "third estate" of the monarchy (as in France), afterwards, in the period of manufacture proper, serving either the semi-feudal or the absolute monarchy as a counterpoise against the nobility, and, in fact, corner stone of the great monarchies in general, the bourgeoisie has at last, since the establishment of Modern Industry and of the world market, conquered for itself, in the modern representative State, exclusive political sway. The executive of the modern State is but a committee for managing the common affairs of the whole bourgeoisie.

13   The bourgeoisie, historically, has played a most revolutionary part.

The bourgeoisie, wherever it has got the upper hand, has put an end to all feudal, patriarchal, idyllic relations. It has pitilessly torn asunder the motley feudal ties that bound man to his "natural superiors," and has left remaining no other nexus between man and man than naked self-interest, than callous "cash payment." It has drowned the most heavenly ecstasies of religious fervour, of chivalrous enthusiasm, of philistine sentimentalism, in the icy water of egotistical calculation. It has resolved personal worth into exchange value, and in place of the numberless indefeasible chartered freedoms, has set up that single, unconscionable freedom — Free Trade. In one word, for exploitation, veiled by religious and political illusions, it has substituted naked, shameless, direct, brutal exploitation.

The bourgeoisie has stripped of its halo every occupation hitherto honoured and looked up to with reverent awe. It has converted the physician, the lawyer, the priest, the poet, the man of science, into its paid wage-labourers.

The bourgeoisie has torn away from the family its sentimental veil, and has reduced the family relation to a mere money relation.

The bourgeoisie has disclosed how it came to pass that the brutal display of vigour in the Middle Ages, which Reactionists so much admire, found its fitting complement in the most slothful indolence. It has been the first to show what man's activity can bring about. It has accomplished wonders far surpassing Egyptian pyramids, Roman aqueducts, and Gothic cathedrals; it has conducted expeditions that put in the shade all former Exoduses of nations and crusades.

The bourgeoisie cannot exist without constantly revolutionising the instruments of production, and thereby the relations of production, and with them the whole relations of society. Conservation of the old modes of production in unaltered form, was, on the contrary, the first condition of existence for all earlier industrial classes. Constant revolutionising of production, uninterrupted disturbance of all social conditions, everlasting uncertainty and agitation distinguish the bourgeois epoch from all earlier ones. All fixed, fast-frozen relations, with their train of ancient and venerable prejudices and opinions, are swept away, all new-formed ones become antiquated before they can ossify. All that is solid melts into air, all that is holy is profaned, and man is at last compelled to face with sober senses, his real conditions of life, and his relations with his kind.

19   The need of a constantly expanding market for its products chases the bourgeoisie over the whole surface of the globe. It must nestle everywhere, settle everywhere, establish connexions everywhere.

20   The bourgeoisie has through its exploitation of the world market given a cosmopolitan character to production and consumption in every country. To the great chagrin of Reactionists, it has drawn from under the feet of industry the national ground on which it stood. All old-established national industries have been destroyed or are daily being destroyed. They are dislodged by new industries, whose introduction becomes a life and death question for all civilised nations, by industries that no longer work up indigenous raw material, but raw material drawn from the remotest zones; industries whose products are consumed, not only at home, but in every quarter of the globe. In place of the old wants, satisfied by the productions of the country, we find new wants, requiring for their satisfaction the products of distant lands and climes. In place of the old local and national seclusion

and self-sufficiency, we have intercourse in every direction, universal inter-dependence of nations. And as in material, so also in intellectual production. The intellectual creations of individual nations become common property. National one-sidedness and narrow-mindedness become more and more impossible, and from the numerous national and local literatures there arises a world-literature.

21 The bourgeoisie, by the rapid improvement of all instruments of production, by the immensely facilitated means of communication, draws all, even the most barbarian, nations into civilisation. The cheap prices of its commodities are the heavy artillery with which it batters down all Chinese walls, with which it forces the barbarians' intensely obstinate hatred of foreigners to capitulate. It compels all nations, on pain of extinction, to adopt the bourgeois mode of production; it compels them to introduce what it calls civilisation into their midst, *i.e.*, to become bourgeois themselves. In one word, it creates a world after its own image.

22 The bourgeoisie has subjected the country to the rule of the towns. It has created enormous cities, has greatly increased the urban population as compared with the rural, and has thus rescued a considerable part of the population from the idiocy of rural life. Just as it has made the country dependent on the towns, so it has made barbarian and semi-barbarian countries dependent on the civilised ones, nations of peasants on nations of bourgeois, the East on the West.

23 The bourgeoisie keeps more and more doing away with the scattered state of the population, of the means of production, and of property. It has agglomerated population, centralised means of production, and has concentrated property in a few hands. The necessary consequence of this was political cen-

tralisation.   Independent, or but loosely connected provinces, with separate interests, laws, governments and systems of taxation, became lumped together into one nation, with one government, one code of laws, one national class-interest, one frontier and one customs-tariff.

24   The bourgeoisie, during its rule of scarce one hundred years, has created more massive and more colossal productive forces than have all preceding generations together.   Subjection of Nature's forces to man, machinery, application of chemistry to industry and agriculture, steam-navigation, railways, electric telegraphs, clearing of whole continents for cultivation, canalisation of rivers, whole populations conjured out of the ground — what earlier century had even a presentiment that such productive forces slumbered in the lap of social labour?

25   We see then: the means of production and of exchange, on whose foundation the bourgeoisie built itself up, were generated in feudal society.   At a certain stage in the development of these means of production and of exchange, the conditions under which feudal society produced and exchanged, the feudal organisation of agriculture and manufacturing industry, in one word, the feudal relations of property became no longer compatible with the already developed productive forces; they became so many fetters.   They had to be burst asunder; they were burst asunder.

26   Into their place stepped free competition, accompanied by a social and political constitution adapted to it, and by the economical and political sway of the bourgeois class.

27   A similar movement is going on before our own eyes. Modern bourgeois society with its relations of production, of exchange and of property, a society that has conjured up such

gigantic means of production and of exchange, is like the sorcerer, who is no longer able to control the powers of the nether world whom he has called up by his spells. For many a decade past the history of industry and commerce is but the history of the revolt of modern productive forces against modern conditions of production, against the property relations that are the conditions for the existence of the bourgeoisie and of its rule. It is enough to mention the commercial crises that by their periodical return put on its trial, each time more threateningly, the existence of the entire bourgeois society. In these crises a great part not only of the existing products, but also of the previously created productive forces, are periodically destroyed. In these crises there breaks out an epidemic that, in all earlier epochs, would have seemed an absurdity — the epidemic of over-production. Society suddenly finds itself put back into a state of momentary barbarism; it appears as if a famine, a universal war of devastation had cut off the supply of every means of subsistence; industry and commerce seem to be destroyed; and why? Because there is too much civilisation, too much means of subsistence, too much industry, too much commerce. The productive forces at the disposal of society no longer tend to further the development of the conditions of bourgeois property; on the contrary, they have become too powerful for these conditions, by which they are fettered, and so soon as they overcome these fetters, they bring disorder into the whole of bourgeois society, endanger the existence of bourgeois property. The conditions of bourgeois society are too narrow to comprise the wealth created by them. And how does the bourgeoisie get over these crises? On the one hand by enforced destruction of a mass of productive forces; on the other, by the conquest of new markets, and by the more thorough exploitation of the old ones. That is to say, by paving the way for more extensive and more destructive crises, and by diminishing the means whereby crises are prevented.

28   The weapons with which the bourgeoisie felled feudalism to the ground are now turned against the bourgeoisie itself.

29   But not only has the bourgeoisie forged the weapons that bring death to itself; it has also called into existence the men who are to wield those weapons — the modern working class — the proletarians.

30   In proportion as the bourgeoisie, *i.e.*, capital, is developed, in the same proportion is the proletariat, the modern working class, developed — a class of labourers, who live only so long as they find work, and who find work only so long as their labour increases capital. These labourers, who must sell themselves piecemeal, are a commodity, like every other article of commerce, and are consequently exposed to all the vicissitudes of competition, to all the fluctuations of the market.

31   Owing to the extensive use of machinery and to division of labour, the work of the proletarians has lost all individual character, and, consequently, all charm for the workman. He becomes an appendage of the machine, and it is only the most simple, most monotonous, and most easily acquired knack, that is required of him. Hence, the cost of production of a workman is restricted, almost entirely, to the means of subsistence that he requires for his maintenance, and for the propagation of his race. But the price of a commodity, and therefore also of labour, is equal to its cost of production. In proportion, therefore, as the repulsiveness of the work increases, the wage decreases. Nay more, in proportion as the use of machinery and division of labour increases, in the

same proportion the burden of toil also increases, whether by prolongation of the working hours, by increase of the work exacted in a given time or by increased speed of the machinery, etc.

Modern industry has converted the little workshop of the patriarchal master into the great factory of the industrial capitalist. Masses of labourers, crowded into the factory, are organised like soldiers. As privates of the industrial army they are placed under the command of a perfect hierarchy of officers and sergeants. Not only are they slaves of the bourgeois class, and of the bourgeois State; they are daily and hourly enslaved by the machine, by the overlooker, and, above all, by the individual bourgeois manufacturer himself. The more openly this despotism proclaims gain to be its end and aim, the more petty, the more hateful and the more embittering it is.

The less the skill and exertion of strength implied in manual labour, in other words, the more modern industry becomes developed, the more is the labour of men superseded by that of women. Differences of age and sex have no longer any distinctive social validity for the working class. All are instruments of labour, more or less expensive to use, according to their age and sex.

No sooner is the exploitation of the labourer by the manufacturer, so far, at an end, that he receives his wages in cash, than he is set upon by the other portions of the bourgeoisie, the landlord, the shopkeeper, the pawnbroker, etc.

The lower strata of the middle class — the small tradespeople, shopkeepers, and retired tradesmen generally, the handicraftsmen and peasants — all these sink gradually into the proletariat, partly because their diminutive capital does not suffice for the scale on which Modern Industry is carried on, and is swamped in the competition with the large capitalists, partly because their specialised skill is rendered worthless by new methods of production. Thus the proletariat is recruited from all classes of the population.

¶ 36 The proletariat goes through various stages of development. With its birth begins its struggle with the bourgeoisie. At first the contest is carried on by individual labourers, then by the workpeople of a factory, then by the operatives of one trade, in one locality, against the individual bourgeois who directly exploits them. They direct their attacks not against the bourgeois conditions of production, but against the instruments of production themselves; they destroy imported wares that compete with their labour, they smash to pieces machinery, they set factories ablaze, they seek to restore by force the vanished status of the workman of the Middle Ages.

¶ 37 At this stage the labourers still form an incoherent mass scattered over the whole country, and broken up by their mutual competition. If anywhere they unite to form more compact bodies, this is not yet the consequence of their own active union, but of the union of the bourgeoisie, which class, in order to attain its own political ends, is compelled to set the whole proletariat in motion, and is moreover yet, for a time, able to do so. At this stage, therefore, the proletarians do not fight their enemies, but the enemies of their enemies, the remnants of absolute monarchy, the landowners, the non-industrial bourgeois, the petty bourgeoisie. Thus the whole historical movement is concentrated in the hands of the bourgeoisie; every victory so obtained is a victory for the bourgeoisie.

8   But with the development of industry the proletariat not only increases in number; it becomes concentrated in greater masses, its strength grows, and it feels that strength more. The various interests and conditions of life within the ranks of the proletariat are more and more equalised, in proportion as machinery obliterates all distinctions of labour, and nearly everywhere reduces wages to the same low level. The growing competition among the bourgeois, and the resulting commercial crises, make the wages of the workers ever more fluctuating. The unceasing improvement of machinery, ever more rapidly developing, makes their livelihood more and more precarious; the collisions between individual workmen and individual bourgeois take more and more the character of collisions between two classes. Thereupon the workers begin to form combinations (Trades' Unions) against the bourgeois; they club together in order to keep up the rate of wages; they found permanent associations in order to make provision beforehand for these occasional revolts. Here and there the contest breaks out into riots.

9   Now and then the workers are victorious, but only for a time. The real fruit of their battles lies, not in the immediate result, but in the ever-expanding union of the workers. This union is helped on by the improved means of communication that are created by modern industry, and that place the workers of different localities in contact with one another. It was just this contact that was needed to centralise the numerous local struggles, all of the same character, into one national struggle between classes. But every class struggle is a political struggle. And that union, to attain which the burghers of the Middle Ages, with their

miserable highways, required centuries, the modern proletarians, thanks to railways, achieve in a few years.

¶ 40   This organisation of the proletarians into a class, and
consequently into a political party, is continually being upset
again by the competition between the workers themselves.
But it ever rises up again, stronger, firmer, mightier.   It
compels legislative recognition of particular interests of the
workers, by taking advantage of the divisions among the
bourgeoisie itself.   Thus the ten-hours' bill in England was
carried.

¶ 41   Altogether collisions between the classes of the old society
further, in many ways, the course of development of the
proletariat.   The bourgeoisie finds itself involved in a constant battle.   At first with the aristocracy; later on, with
those portions of the bourgeoisie itself, whose interests have
become antagonistic to the progress of industry; at all times,
with the bourgeoisie of foreign countries.   In all these battles it sees itself compelled to appeal to the proletariat, to
ask for its help, and thus, to drag it into the political arena.
The bourgeoisie itself, therefore, supplies the proletariat
with its own elements of political and general education,
in other words, it furnishes the proletariat with weapons
for fighting the bourgeoisie.

¶ 42   Further, as we have already seen, entire sections of the
ruling classes are, by the advance of industry, precipitated
into the proletariat, or are at least threatened in their conditions of existence.   These also supply the proletariat with
fresh elements of enlightenment and progress.

¶ 43   Finally, in times when the class struggle nears the decisive
hour, the process of dissolution going on within the ruling
class, in fact within the whole range of old society, assumes

such a violent, glaring character, that a small section of the ruling class cuts itself adrift, and joins the revolutionary class, the class that holds the future in its hands. Just as, therefore, at an earlier period, a section of the nobility went over to the bourgeoisie, so now a portion of the bourgeoisie goes over to the proletariat, and in particular, a portion of the bourgeois ideologists, who have raised themselves to the level of comprehending theoretically the historical movement as a whole.

Of all the classes that stand face to face with the bourgeoisie to-day, the proletariat alone is a really revolutionary class. The other classes decay and finally disappear in the face of modern industry; the proletariat is its special and essential product.

The lower middle class, the small manufacturer, the shop-keeper, the artisan, the peasant, all these fight against the bourgeoisie, to save from extinction their existence as fractions of the middle class. They are therefore not revolutionary, but conservative. Nay more, they are reactionary, for they try to roll back the wheel of history. If by chance they are revolutionary, they are so only in view of their impending transfer into the proletariat, they thus defend not their present, but their future interests, they desert their own standpoint to place themselves at that of the proletariat.

The "dangerous class," the social scum, that passively rotting mass thrown off by the lowest layers of old society, may, here and there, be swept into the movement by a proletarian revolution; its conditions of life, however, prepare it far more for the part of a bribed tool of reactionary intrigue.

In the conditions of the proletariat, those of old society

at large are already virtually swamped. The proletarian is without property; his relation to his wife and children has no longer anything in common with the bourgeois family-relations; modern industrial labour, modern subjection to capital, the same in England as in France, in America as in Germany, has stripped him of every trace of national character. Law, morality, religion, are to him so many bourgeois prejudices, behind which lurk in ambush just as many bourgeois interests.

48   All the preceding classes that got the upper hand, sought to fortify their already acquired status by subjecting society at large to their conditions of appropriation. The proletarians cannot become masters of the productive forces of society, except by abolishing their own previous mode of appropriation, and thereby also every other previous mode of appropriation. They have nothing of their own to secure and to fortify; their mission is to destroy all previous securities for, and insurances of, individual property.

49   All previous historical movements were movements of minorities, or in the interest of minorities. The proletarian movement is the self-conscious, independent movement of the immense majority, in the interest of the immense majority. The proletariat, the lowest stratum of our present society, cannot stir, cannot raise itself up, without the whole superincumbent strata of official society being sprung into the air.

50   Though not in substance, yet in form, the struggle of the proletariat with the bourgeoisie is at first a national struggle. The proletariat of each country must, of course, first of all settle matters with its own bourgeoisie.

51   In depicting the most general phases of the development of the proletariat, we traced the more or less veiled civil

war, raging within existing society, up to the point where that war breaks out into open revolution, and where the violent overthrow of the bourgeoisie lays the foundation for the sway of the proletariat.

Hitherto, every form of society has been based, as we have already seen, on the antagonism of oppressing and oppressed classes. But in order to oppress a class, certain conditions must be assured to it under which it can, at least, continue its slavish existence. The serf, in the period of serfdom, raised himself to membership in the commune, just as the petty bourgeois, under the yoke of feudal absolutism, managed to develop into a bourgeois. The modern labourer, on the contrary, instead of rising with the progress of industry, sinks deeper and deeper below the conditions of existence of his own class. He becomes a pauper, and pauperism develops more rapidly than population and wealth. And here it becomes evident, that the bourgeoisie is unfit any longer to be the ruling class in society, and to impose its conditions of existence upon society as an over-riding law. It is unfit to rule because it is incompetent to assure an existence to its slave within his slavery, because it cannot help letting him sink into such a state, that it has to feed him, instead of being fed by him. Society can no longer live under this bourgeoisie, in other words, its existence is no longer compatible with society.

The essential condition for the existence, and for the sway of the bourgeois class, is the formation and augmentation of capital; the condition for capital is wage-labour. Wage-labour rests exclusively on competition between the labourers. The advance of industry, whose involuntary promoter is the bourgeoisie, replaces the isolation of the labourers, due to competition, by their revolutionary combination, due to association. The development of Modern Industry, therefore, cuts from under its feet the very foundation on which the bourgeoisie produces and appropriates products. What the bourgeoisie, therefore, produces, above all, are its own grave-diggers. Its fall and the victory of the proletariat are equally inevitable.

II
PROLETARIANS AND COMMUNISTS

In what relation do the Communists stand to the proletarians as a whole?

The Communists do not form a separate party opposed to other working-class parties.

They have no interests separate and apart from those of the proletariat as a whole.

They do not set up any sectarian principles of their own, by which to shape and mould the proletarian movement.

The Communists are distinguished from the other working-class parties by this only: 1. In the national struggles of the proletarians of the different countries, they point out and bring to the front the common interests of the entire proletariat, independently of all nationality. 2. In the various stages of development which the struggle of the working class against the bourgeoisie has to pass through, they always and everywhere represent the interests of the movement as a whole.

¶ 59   The Communists, therefore, are on the one hand, practically, the most advanced and resolute section of the working-class parties of every country, that section which pushes forward all others; on the other hand, theoretically, they have over the great mass of the proletariat the advantage of clearly understanding the line of march, the conditions, and the ultimate general results of the proletarian movement.

¶ 60   The immediate aim of the Communists is the same as that of all the other proletarian parties: formation of the proletariat into a class, overthrow of the bourgeois supremacy, conquest of political power by the proletariat.

¶ 61   The theoretical conclusions of the Communists are in no way based on ideas or principles that have been invented, or discovered, by this or that would-be universal reformer.

¶ 62   They merely express, in general terms, actual relations springing from an existing class struggle, from a historical movement going on under our very eyes. The abolition of existing property relations is not at all a distinctive feature of Communism.

¶ 63   All property relations in the past have continually been subject to historical change consequent upon the change in historical conditions.

¶ 64   The French Revolution, for example, abolished feudal property in favour of bourgeois property.

¶ 65   The distinguishing feature of Communism is not the abolition of property generally, but the abolition of bourgeois property.   But modern bourgeois private property is the final and most complete expression of the system of producing and appropriating products, that is based on class antagonisms, on the exploitation of the many by the few.

¶ 66   In this sense, the theory of the Communists may be summed up in the single sentence: Abolition of private property.

We Communists have been reproached with the desire of abolishing the right of personally acquiring property as the fruit of a man's own labour, which property is alleged to be the ground work of all personal freedom, activity and independence.

Hard-won, self-acquired, self-earned property! Do you mean the property of the petty artisan and of the small peasant, a form of property that preceded the bourgeois form? There is no need to abolish that; the development of industry has to a great extent already destroyed it, and is still destroying it daily.

Or do you mean modern bourgeois private property?

But does wage-labour create any property for the labourer? Not a bit. It creates capital, *i.e.*, that kind of property which exploits wage-labour, and which cannot increase except upon condition of begetting a new supply of wage-labour for fresh exploitation. Property, in its present form, is based on the antagonism of capital and wage-labour. Let us examine both sides of this antagonism.

To be a capitalist, is to have not only a purely personal, but a social *status* in production. Capital is a collective product, and only by the united action of many members, nay, in the last resort, only by the united action of all members of society, can it be set in motion.

Capital is, therefore, not a personal, it is a social power.

When, therefore, capital is converted into common property, into the property of all members of society, personal property is not thereby transformed into social property. It is only the social character of the property that is changed. It loses its class character.

Let us now take wage-labour.

¶ 75   The average price of wage-labour is the minimum wage, *i.e.*, that quantum of the means of subsistence, which is absolutely requisite to keep the labourer in bare existence as a labourer. What, therefore, the wage-labourer appropriates by means of his labour, merely suffices to prolong and reproduce a bare existence. We by no means intend to abolish this personal appropriation of the products of labour, an appropriation that is made for the maintenance and reproduction of human life, and that leaves no surplus wherewith to command the labour of others. All that we want to do away with is the miserable character of this appropriation, under which the labourer lives merely to increase capital, and is allowed to live only in so far as the interest of the ruling class requires it.

¶ 76   In bourgeois society, living labour is but a means to increase accumulated labour. In Communist society, accumulated labour is but a means to widen, to enrich, to promote the existence of the labourer.

¶ 77   In bourgeois society, therefore, the past dominates the present; in Communist society, the present dominates the past. In bourgeois society capital is independent and has individuality, while the living person is dependent and has no individuality.

¶ 78   And the abolition of this state of things is called by the bourgeois, abolition of individuality and freedom! And rightly so. The abolition of bourgeois individuality, bourgeois independence, and bourgeois freedom is undoubtedly aimed at.

¶ 79   By freedom is meant, under the present bourgeois conditions of production, free trade, free selling and buying.

¶ 80   But if selling and buying disappears, free selling and buying disappears also. This talk about free selling and buying, and all the other "brave words" of our bourgeoisie about freedom in general, have a meaning, if any, only in contrast with restricted selling and buying, with the fettered traders of the Middle Ages, but have no meaning when opposed to the Communistic abolition of buying and selling, of the bourgeois conditions of production, and of the bourgeoisie itself.

You are horrified at our intending to do away with private property. But in your existing society, private property is already done away with for nine-tenths of the population; its existence for the few is solely due to its non-existence in the hands of those nine-tenths. You reproach us, therefore, with intending to do away with a form of property, the necessary condition for whose existence is, the non-existence of any property for the immense majority of society.

In one word, you reproach us with intending to do away with your property. Precisely so; that is just what we intend.

From the moment when labour can no longer be converted into capital, money, or rent, into a social power capable of being monopolised, *i.e.,* from the moment when individual property can no longer be transformed into bourgeois property, into capital, from that moment, you say, individuality vanishes.

You must, therefore, confess that by "individual" you mean no other person than the bourgeois, than the middle-class owner of property. This person must, indeed, be swept out of the way, and made impossible.

Communism deprives no man of the power to appropriate the products of society; all that it does is to deprive him of the power to subjugate the labour of others by means of such appropriation.

¶ 86 It has been objected that upon the abolition of private property all work will cease, and universal laziness will overtake us.

¶ 87 According to this, bourgeois society ought long ago to have gone to the dogs through sheer idleness; for those of its members who work, acquire nothing, and those who acquire anything, do not work. The whole of this objection is but another expression of the tautology: that there can no longer be any wage-labour when there is no longer any capital.

¶ 88 All objections urged against the Communistic mode of producing and appropriating material products, have, in the same way, been urged against the Communistic modes of producing and appropriating intellectual products. Just as, to the bourgeois, the disappearance of class property is the disappearance of production itself, so the disappearance of class culture is to him identical with the disappearance of all culture.

¶ 89 That culture, the loss of which he laments, is, for the enormous majority, a mere training to act as a machine.

¶ 90 But don't wrangle with us so long as you apply, to our intended abolition of bourgeois property, the standard of your bourgeois notions of freedom, culture, law, etc. Your very ideas are but the outgrowth of the conditions of your bourgeois production and bourgeois property, just as your jurisprudence is but the will of your class made into a law for all, a will, whose essential character and direction are determined by the economical conditions of existence of your class.

¶ 91 The selfish misconception that induces you to transform into eternal laws of nature and of reason, the social forms springing from your present mode of production and form of property — historical relations that rise and disappear in the progress of production — this misconception you share with every ruling class that has preceded you. What you see clearly in the case of ancient property, what you admit in the case of feudal property, you are of course forbidden to admit in the case of your own bourgeois form of property.

Abolition of the family! Even the most radical flare up at this infamous proposal of the Communists.

On what foundation is the present family, the bourgeois family, based? On capital, on private gain. In its completely developed form this family exists only among the bourgeoisie. But this state of things finds its complement in the practical absence of the family among the proletarians, and in public prostitution.

The bourgeois family will vanish as a matter of course when its complement vanishes, and both will vanish with the vanishing of capital.

Do you charge us with wanting to stop the exploitation of children by their parents? To this crime we plead guilty.

But, you will say, we destroy the most hallowed of relations, when we replace home education by social.

And your education! Is not that also social, and determined by the social conditions under which you educate, by the intervention, direct or indirect, of society, by means of schools, etc.? The Communists have not invented the intervention of society in education; they do but seek to alter the character of that intervention, and to rescue education from the influence of the ruling class.

The bourgeois clap-trap about the family and education, about the hallowed co-relation of parent and child, becomes all the more disgusting, the more, by the action of Modern

Industry, all family ties among the proletarians are torn asunder, and their children transformed into simple articles of commerce and instruments of labour.

99   **But you Communists would introduce community of women,** screams the whole bourgeoisie in chorus.

100   The bourgeois sees in his wife a mere instrument of production. He hears that the instruments of production are to be exploited in common, and, naturally, can come to no other conclusion than that the lot of being common to all will likewise fall to the women.

101   He has not even a suspicion that the real point aimed at is to do away with the status of women as mere instruments of production.

102   For the rest, nothing is more ridiculous than the virtuous indignation of our bourgeois at the community of women which, they pretend, is to be openly and officially established by the Communists. The Communists have no need to introduce community of women; it has existed almost from time immemorial.

103   Our bourgeois, not content with having the wives and daughters of their proletarians at their disposal, not to speak of common prostitutes, take the greatest pleasure in seducing each others' wives.

104   Bourgeois marriage is in reality a system of wives in common and thus, at the most, what the Communists might possibly be reproached with, is that they desire to introduce, in substitution for a hypocritically concealed, an openly legalised community of women. For the rest, it is self-evident that the abolition of the present system of production must bring with it the abolition of the community of women springing from that system, *i.e.,* of prostitution both public and private.

5   The Communists are further reproached with desiring to abolish countries and nationality.

6   The working men have no country. We cannot take from them what they have not got. Since the proletariat must first of all acquire political supremacy, must rise to be the leading class of the nation, must constitute itself *the* nation, it is, so far, itself national, though not in the bourgeois sense of the word.

7   National differences and antagonisms between peoples are daily more and more vanishing, owing to the development of the bourgeoisie, to freedom of commerce, to the world market, to uniformity in the mode of production and in the conditions of life corresponding thereto.

8   The supremacy of the proletariat will cause them to vanish still faster. United action, of the leading civilised countries at least, is one of the first conditions for the emancipation of the proletariat.

9   In proportion as the exploitation of one individual by another is put an end to, the exploitation of one nation by another will also be put an end to. In proportion as the antagonism between classes within the nation vanishes, the hostility of one nation to another will come to an end.

0   The charges against Communism made from a religious, a philosophical, and, generally, from an ideological standpoint, are not deserving of serious examination.

1   Does it require deep intuition to comprehend that man's ideas, views and conceptions, in one word, man's consciousness, changes with every change in the conditions of his material existence, in his social relations and in his social life?

2   What else does the history of ideas prove, than that intellectual production changes its character in proportion

as material production is changed?   The ruling ideas of each age have ever been the ideas of its ruling class.

113   When people speak of ideas that revolutionise society, they do but express the fact, that within the old society, the elements of a new one have been created, and that the dissolution of the old ideas keeps even pace with the dissolution of the old conditions of existence.

114   When the ancient world was in its last throes, the ancient religions were overcome by Christianity.   When Christian ideas succumbed in the 18th century to rationalist ideas, feudal society fought its death-battle with the then revolutionary bourgeoisie.   The ideas of religious liberty and freedom of conscience, merely gave expression to the sway of free competition within the domain of knowledge.

115   "Undoubtedly," it will be said, "religious, moral, philosophical and juridical ideas have been modified in the course of historical development.   But religion, morality, philosophy, political science, and law, constantly survived this change."

116   "There are, besides, eternal truths, such as Freedom, Justice, etc., that are common to all states of society.   But Communism abolishes eternal truths, it abolishes all religion, and all morality, instead of constituting them on a new basis; it therefore acts in contradiction to all past historical experience."

117   What does this accusation reduce itself to?   The history of all past society has consisted in the development of class antagonisms, antagonisms that assumed different forms at different epochs.

118   But whatever form they may have taken, one fact is common to all past ages, *viz.*, the exploitation of one part of society by the other.   No wonder, then, that the social con-

sciousness of past ages, despite all the multiplicity and variety it displays, moves within certain common forms, or general ideas, which cannot completely vanish except with the total disappearance of class antagonisms.

119 The Communist revolution is the most radical rupture with traditional property relations; no wonder that its development involves the most radical rupture with traditional ideas.

120 But let us have done with the bourgeois objections to Communism.

121 We have seen above, that the first step in the revolution by the working class, is to raise the proletariat to the position of ruling class, to win the battle of democracy.

122 The proletariat will use its political supremacy to wrest, by degrees, all capital from the bourgeoisie, to centralise all instruments of production in the hands of the State, *i.e.*, of the proletariat organised as the ruling class; and to increase the total of productive forces as rapidly as possible.

123 Of course, in the beginning, this cannot be effected except by means of despotic inroads on the rights of property, and on the conditions of bourgeois production; by means of measures, therefore, which appear economically insufficient and untenable, but which, in the course of the movement, outstrip themselves, necessitate further inroads upon the old social order, and are unavoidable as a means of entirely revolutionising the mode of production.

124 These measures will of course be different in different countries.

125 Nevertheless in the most advanced countries, the following will be pretty generally applicable.

 1. Abolition of property in land and application of all rents of land to public purposes.

 2. A heavy progressive or graduated income tax.

3.   Abolition of all right of inheritance.

4.   Confiscation of the property of all emigrants and rebels.

5.   Centralisation of credit in the hands of the State, by means of a national bank with State capital and an exclusive monopoly.

6.   Centralisation of the means of communication and transport in the hands of the State.

7.   Extension of factories and instruments of production owned by the State; the bringing into cultivation of waste lands, and the improvement of the soil generally in accordance with a common plan.

8.   Equal liability of all to labour.   Establishment of industrial armies, especially for agriculture.

9.   Combination of agriculture with manufacturing industries; gradual abolition of the distinction between town and country, by a more equable distribution of the population over the country.

10.   Free education for all children in public schools. Abolition of children's factory labour in its present form. Combination of education with industrial production, etc., etc.

26   When, in the course of development, class distinctions have disappeared, and all production has been concentrated in the hands of a vast association of the whole nation, the public power will lose its political character.   Political power, properly so called, is merely the organised power of one class for oppressing another.   If the proletariat during its contest with the bourgeoisie is compelled, by the force of circumstances, to organise itself as a class, if, by means of a revolution, it makes itself the ruling class, and, as such, sweeps away by force the old conditions of production, then it will, along with these conditions, have swept away the conditions for the

existence of class antagonisms and of classes generally, and will thereby have abolished its own supremacy as a class.

27   In place of the old bourgeois society, with its classes and class antagonisms, we shall have an association, in which the free development of each is the condition for the free development of all.

III

SOCIALIST AND COMMUNIST LITERATURE

---

1. REACTIONARY SOCIALISM

a. Feudal Socialism

28 Owing to their historical position, it became the vocation of the aristocracies of France and England to write pamphlets against modern bourgeois society. In the French revolution of July, 1830, and in the English reform agitation, these aristocracies again succumbed to the hateful upstart. Thenceforth, a serious political contest was altogether out of the question. A literary battle alone remained possible. But even in the domain of literature the old cries of the restoration period had become impossible.

29 In order to arouse sympathy, the aristocracy were obliged to lose sight, apparently, of their own interests, and to formulate their indictment against the bourgeoisie in the interest of the exploited working class alone. Thus the aristocracy

176

took their revenge by singing lampoons on their new master, and whispering in his ears sinister prophecies of coming catastrophe.

0   In this way arose feudal Socialism: half lamentation, half lampoon; half echo of the past, half menace of the future; at times, by its bitter, witty and incisive criticism, striking the bourgeoisie to the very heart's core; but always ludicrous in its effect, through total incapacity to comprehend the march of modern history.

1   The aristocracy, in order to rally the people to them, waved the proletarian alms-bag in front for a banner. But the people, so often as it joined them, saw on their hindquarters the old feudal coats of arms, and deserted with loud and irreverent laughter.

2   One section of the French Legitimists and "Young England" exhibited this spectacle.

3   In pointing out that their mode of exploitation was different to that of the bourgeoisie, the feudalists forget that they exploited under circumstances and conditions that were quite different, and that are now antiquated. In showing that, under their rule, the modern proletariat never existed, they forget that the modern bourgeoisie is the necessary offspring of their own form of society.

4   For the rest, so little do they conceal the reactionary character of their criticism that their chief accusation against the bourgeoisie amounts to this, that under the bourgeois *régime* a class is being developed, which is destined to cut up root and branch the old order of society.

5   What they upbraid the bourgeoisie with is not so much that it creates a proletariat, as that it creates a *revolutionary* proletariat.

136   In political practice, therefore, they join in all coercive measures against the working class; and in ordinary life, despite their high-falutin phrases, they stoop to pick up the golden apples dropped from the tree of industry, and to barter truth, love, and honour for traffic in wool, beetroot-sugar, and potato spirits.

137   As the parson has ever gone hand in hand with the landlord, so has Clerical Socialism with Feudal Socialism.

138   Nothing is easier than to give Christian asceticism a Socialist tinge.   Has not Christianity declaimed against private property, against marriage, against the State?   Has it not preached in the place of these, charity and poverty, celibacy and mortification of the flesh, monastic life and Mother Church?   Christian Socialism is but the holy water with which the priest consecrates the heart-burnings of the aristocrat.

b.   Petty-Bourgeois Socialism

139   The feudal aristocracy was not the only class that was ruined by the bourgeoisie, not the only class whose conditions of existence pined and perished in the atmosphere of modern bourgeois society.   The mediaeval burgesses and the small peasant proprietors were the precursors of the modern bourgeoisie.   In those countries which are but little developed, industrially and commercially, these two classes still vegetate side by side with the rising bourgeoisie.

140   In countries where modern civilisation has become fully developed, a new class of petty bourgeois has been formed, fluctuating between proletariat and bourgeoisie, and ever renewing itself as a supplementary part of bourgeois society. The individual members of this class, however, are being

constantly hurled down into the proletariat by the action of competition, and, as modern industry develops, they even see the moment approaching when they will completely disappear as an independent section of modern society, to be replaced, in manufactures, agriculture and commerce, by overlookers, bailiffs and shopmen.

In countries like France, where the peasants constitute far more than half of the population, it was natural that writers who sided with the proletariat against the bourgeoisie, should use, in their criticism of the bourgeois *régime*, the standard of the peasant and petty bourgeois, and from the standpoint of these intermediate classes should take up the cudgels for the working class. Thus arose petty-bourgeois Socialism. Sismondi was the head of this school, not only in France but also in England.

This school of Socialism dissected with great acuteness the contradictions in the conditions of modern production. It laid bare the hypocritical apologies of economists. It proved, incontrovertibly, the disastrous effects of machinery and division of labour; the concentration of capital and land in a few hands; overproduction and crises; it pointed out the inevitable ruin of the petty bourgeois and peasant, the misery of the proletariat, the anarchy in production, the crying inequalities in the distribution of wealth, the industrial war of extermination between nations, the dissolution of old moral bonds, of the old family relations, of the old nationalities.

In its positive aims, however, this form of Socialism aspires either to restoring the old means of production and of exchange, and with them the old property relations, and the old society, or to cramping the modern means of production and of exchange, within the framework of the old property relations that have been, and were bound to be, exploded by those means. In either case, it is both reactionary and Utopian.

144   Its last words are: corporate guilds for manufacture; patriarchal relations in agriculture.

145   Ultimately, when stubborn historical facts had dispersed all intoxicating effects of self-deception, this form of Socialism ended in a miserable fit of the blues.

c.   German, or "True," Socialism

146   The Socialist and Communist literature of France, a literature that originated under the pressure of a bourgeoisie in power, and that was the expression of the struggle against this power, was introduced into Germany at a time when the bourgeoisie, in that country, had just begun its contest with feudal absolutism.

147   German philosophers, would-be philosophers, and *beaux esprits,* eagerly seized on this literature, only forgetting, that when these writings immigrated from France into Germany, French social conditions had not immigrated along with them. In contact with German social conditions, this French literature lost all its immediate practical significance, and assumed a purely literary aspect. Thus, to the German philosophers of the Eighteenth Century, the demands of the first French Revolution were nothing more than the demands of "Practical Reason" in general, and the utterance of the will of the revolutionary French bourgeoisie signified in their eyes the laws of pure Will, of Will as it was bound to be, of true human Will generally.

148   The work of the German *literati* consisted solely in bringing the new French ideas into harmony with their ancient

philosophical conscience, or rather, in annexing the French ideas without deserting their own philosophic point of view.

This annexation took place in the same way in which a foreign language is appropriated, namely, by translation.

It is well known how the monks wrote silly lives of Catholic Saints *over* the manuscripts on which the classical works of ancient heathendom had been written. The German *literati* reversed this process with the profane French literature. They wrote their philosophical nonsense beneath the French original. For instance, beneath the French criticism of the economic functions of money, they wrote "Alienation of Humanity," and beneath the French criticism of the bourgeois State they wrote, "Dethronement of the Category of the General," and so forth.

The introduction of these philosophical phrases at the back of the French historical criticisms they dubbed "Philosophy of Action," "True Socialism," "German Science of Socialism," "Philosophical Foundation of Socialism," and so on.

The French Socialist and Communist literature was thus completely emasculated. And, since it ceased in the hands of the German to express the struggle of one class with the other, he felt conscious of having overcome "French one-sidedness" and of representing, not true requirements, but the requirements of Truth; not the interests of the proletariat, but the interests of Human Nature, of Man in general, who belongs to no class, has no reality, who exists only in the misty realm of philosophical fantasy.

This German Socialism, which took its school-boy task so seriously and solemnly, and extolled its poor stock-in-trade in such mountebank fashion, meanwhile gradually lost its pedantic innocence.

The fight of the German, and, especially, of the Prussian

bourgeoisie, against feudal aristocracy and absolute monarchy, in other words, the liberal movement, became more earnest.

¶ 155   By this, the long-wished-for opportunity was offered to "True" Socialism of confronting the political movement with the Socialist demands, of hurling the traditional anathemas against liberalism, against representative government, against bourgeois competition, bourgeois freedom of the press, bourgeois legislation, bourgeois liberty and equality, and of preaching to the masses that they had nothing to gain, and everything to lose, by this bourgeois movement. German Socialism forgot, in the nick of time, that the French criticism, whose silly echo it was, presupposed the existence of modern bourgeois society, with its corresponding economic conditions of existence, and the political constitution adapted thereto, the very things whose attainment was the object of the pending struggle in Germany.

¶ 156   To the absolute governments, with their following of parsons, professors, country squires and officials, it served as a welcome scarecrow against the threatening bourgeoisie.

¶ 157   It was a sweet finish after the bitter pills of floggings and bullets with which these same governments, just at that time, dosed the German working-class risings.

¶ 158   While this "True" Socialism thus served the governments as a weapon for fighting the German bourgeoisie, it, at the same time, directly represented a reactionary interest, the interest of the German Philistines. In Germany the *petty-bourgeois* class, a relic of the 16th century, and since then constantly cropping up again under various forms, is the real social basis of the existing state of things.

¶ 159   To preserve this class is to preserve the existing state of things in Germany. The industrial and political supremacy of the bourgeoisie threatens it with certain destruction; on the one hand, from the concentration of capital; on the other, from the rise of a revolutionary proletariat. "True" Socialism appeared to kill these two birds with one stone. It spread like an epidemic.

The robe of speculative cobwebs, embroidered with flowers of rhetoric, steeped in the dew of sickly sentiment, this transcendental robe in which the German Socialists wrapped their sorry "eternal truths," all skin and bone, served to wonderfully increase the sale of their goods amongst such a public.

And on its part, German Socialism recognised, more and more, its own calling as the bombastic representative of the petty-bourgeois Philistine.

It proclaimed the German nation to be the model nation, and the German petty Philistine to be the typical man. To every villainous meanness of this model man it gave a hidden, higher, Socialistic interpretation, the exact contrary of its real character. It went to the extreme length of directly opposing the "brutally destructive" tendency of Communism, and of proclaiming its supreme and impartial contempt of all class struggles. With very few exceptions, all the so-called Socialist and Communist publications that now (1847) circulate in Germany belong to the domain of this foul and enervating literature.

2. CONSERVATIVE, OR BOURGEOIS, SOCIALISM

A part of the bourgeoisie is desirous of redressing social grievances, in order to secure the continued existence of bourgeois society.

¶ 164   To this section belong economists, philanthropists, humanitarians, improvers of the condition of the working class, organisers of charity, members of societies for the prevention of cruelty to animals, temperance fanatics, hole-and-corner reformers of every imaginable kind. This form of Socialism has, moreover, been worked out into complete systems.

¶ 165   We may cite Proudhon's *Philosophie de la Misère* as an example of this form.

¶ 166   The Socialistic bourgeois want all the advantages of modern social conditions without the struggles and dangers necessarily resulting therefrom. They desire the existing state of society minus its revolutionary and disintegrating elements. They wish for a bourgeoisie without a proletariat. The bourgeoisie naturally conceives the world in which it is supreme to be the best; and bourgeois Socialism develops this comfortable conception into various more or less complete systems. In requiring the proletariat to carry out such a system, and thereby to march straightway into the social New Jerusalem, it but requires in reality, that the proletariat should remain within the bounds of existing society, but should cast away all its hateful ideas concerning the bourgeoisie.

¶ 167   A second and more practical, but less systematic, form of this Socialism sought to depreciate every revolutionary movement in the eyes of the working class, by showing that no mere political reform, but only a change in the material conditions of existence, in economical relations, could be of any advantage to them. By changes in the material conditions of existence, this form of Socialism, however, by no means understands abolition of the bourgeois relations of production, an abolition that can be effected only by a revolution, but administrative reforms, based on the continued existence of these relations; reforms, therefore, that in no respect affect the relations between capital and labour, but, at the best, lessen the cost, and simplify the administrative work, of bourgeois government.

38   Bourgeois Socialism attains adequate expression, when, and only when, it becomes a mere figure of speech.

39   Free trade: for the benefit of the working class. Protective duties: for the benefit of the working class. Prison Reform: for the benefit of the working class. This is the last word and the only seriously meant word of bourgeois Socialism.

70   It is summed up in the phrase: the bourgeois is a bourgeois — for the benefit of the working class.

3. CRITICAL-UTOPIAN SOCIALISM AND COMMUNISM

71   We do not here refer to that literature which, in every great modern revolution, has always given voice to the demands of the proletariat, such as the writings of Babeuf and others.

72   The first direct attempts of the proletariat to attain its own ends, made in times of universal excitement, when feudal society was being overthrown, these attempts necessarily failed, owing to the then undeveloped state of the proletariat, as well as to the absence of the economic conditions for its emancipation, conditions that had yet to be produced, and could be produced by the impending bourgeois epoch alone. The revolutionary literature that accompanied these first movements of the proletariat had necessarily a reactionary character. It inculcated universal asceticism and social levelling in its crudest form.

73   The Socialist and Communist systems properly so called, those of St. Simon, Fourier, Owen and others, spring into existence in the early undeveloped period, described above, of the struggle between proletariat and bourgeoisie (see Section I. Bourgeois and Proletarians).

74   The founders of these systems see, indeed, the class antagonisms, as well as the action of the decomposing elements in the prevailing form of society.   But the proletariat, as yet in its infancy, offers to them the spectacle of a class without any historical initiative or any independent political movement.

75   Since the development of class antagonism keeps even pace with the development of industry, the economic situation, as they find it, does not as yet offer to them the material conditions for the emancipation of the proletariat.   They therefore search after a new social science, after new social laws, that are to create these conditions.

76   Historical action is to yield to their personal inventive action, historically created conditions of emancipation to fantastic ones, and the gradual, spontaneous class-organisation of the proletariat to an organisation of society specially contrived by these inventors.   Future history resolves itself, in their eyes, into the propaganda and the practical carrying out of their social plans.

77   In the formation of their plans they are conscious of caring chiefly for the interests of the working class, as being the most suffering class.   Only from the point of view of being the most suffering class does the proletariat exist for them.

178   The undeveloped state of the class struggle, as well as their own surroundings, causes Socialists of this kind to consider

themselves far superior to all class antagonisms. They want to improve the condition of every member of society, even that of the most favoured. Hence, they habitually appeal to society at large, without distinction of class; nay, by preference, to the ruling class. For how can people, when once they understand their system, fail to see in it the best possible plan of the best possible state of society?

9   Hence, they reject all political, and especially all revolutionary, action; they wish to attain their ends by peaceful means, and endeavour, by small experiments, necessarily doomed to failure, and by the force of example, to pave the way for the new social Gospel.

0   Such fantastic pictures of future society, painted at a time when the proletariat is still in a very undeveloped state and has but a fantastic conception of its own position, correspond with[58] the first instinctive yearnings of that class for a general reconstruction of society.

1   But these Socialist and Communist publications contain also a critical element. They attack every principle of existing society. Hence they are full of the most valuable materials for the enlightenment of the working class. The practical measures proposed in them — such as the abolition of the distinction between town and country, of the family, of the carrying on of industries for the account of private individuals, and of the wage system, the proclamation of social harmony, the conversion of the functions of the State into a mere superintendence of production, all these proposals point solely to the disappearance of class antagonisms which were, at that time, only just cropping up, and which, in these publications, are recognised in their earliest, indis-

tinct and undefined forms only. These proposals, therefore, are of a purely Utopian character.

182 The significance of Critical-Utopian Socialism and Communism bears an inverse relation to historical development. In proportion as the modern class struggle develops and takes definite shape, this fantastic standing apart from the contest, these fantastic attacks on it, lose all practical value and all theoretical justification. Therefore, although the originators of these systems were, in many respects, revolutionary, their disciples have, in every case, formed mere reactionary sects. They hold fast by the original views of their masters, in opposition to the progressive historical development of the proletariat. They, therefore, endeavour, and that consistently, to deaden the class struggle and to reconcile the class antagonisms. They still dream of experimental realisation of their social Utopias, of founding isolated *"phalanstères,"* of establishing "Home Colonies," of setting up a "Little Icaria" — duodecimo editions of the New Jerusalem — and to realise all these castles in the air, they are compelled to appeal to the feelings and purses of the bourgeois. By degrees they sink into the category of the reactionary conservative Socialists depicted above, differing from these only by more systematic pedantry, and by their fanatical and superstitious belief in the miraculous effects of their social science.

183 They, therefore, violently oppose all political action on the part of the working class; such action, according to them, can only result from blind unbelief in the new Gospel.

184 The Owenites in England, and the Fourierists in France, respectively oppose the Chartists and the *Réformistes*.

IV

POSITION OF THE COMMUNIST IN RELATION TO THE VARIOUS EXISTING OPPOSITION PARTIES

---

185   Section II has made clear the relations of the Communists to the existing working-class parties, such as the Chartists in England and the Agrarian Reformers in America.

186   The Communists fight for the attainment of the immediate aims, for the enforcement of the momentary interests of the working class; but in the movement of the present, they also represent and take care of the future of that movement. In France the Communists ally themselves with the Social-Democrats, against the conservative and radical bourgeoisie, reserving, however, the right to take up a critical position in regard to phrases and illusions traditionally handed down from the great Revolution.

7   In Switzerland they support the Radicals, without losing sight of the fact that this party consists of antagonistic elements, partly of Democratic Socialists, in the French sense, partly of radical bourgeois.

8   In Poland they support the party that insists on an agrarian revolution as the prime condition for national emancipation, that party which fomented the insurrection of Cracow in 1846.

9   In Germany they fight with the bourgeoisie whenever it acts in a revolutionary way, against the absolute monarchy, the feudal squirearchy, and the petty bourgeoisie.

0   But they never cease, for a single instant, to instil into the working class the clearest possible recognition of the hostile antagonism between bourgeoisie and proletariat, in order that the German workers may straightway use, as so many weapons against the bourgeoisie, the social and political conditions that the bourgeoisie must necessarily introduce along with its supremacy, and in order that, after the fall of the reactionary classes in Germany, the fight against the bourgeoisie itself may immediately begin.

1   The Communists turn their attention chiefly to Germany, because that country is on the eve of a bourgeois revolution that is bound to be carried out under more advanced conditions of European civilisation, and with a much more developed proletariat, than that of England was in the seventeenth, and of France in the eighteenth century, and because the bourgeois revolution in Germany will be but the prelude to an immediately following proletarian revolution.

2   In short, the Communists everywhere support every revolutionary movement against the existing social and political order of things.

193   In all these movements they bring to the front, as the leading question in each, the property question, no matter what its degree of development at the time.

94   Finally, they labour everywhere for the union and agreement of the democratic parties of all countries.

195   The Communists disdain to conceal their views and aims. They openly declare that their ends can be attained only by the forcible overthrow of all existing social conditions. Let the ruling classes tremble at a Communistic revolution. The proletarians have nothing to lose but their chains. They have a world to win.

196   WORKING MEN OF ALL COUNTRIES, UNITE!

Schematic Overview

¶ 31-33		Proletarian work is dehumanized and meaningless.
¶ 34		Proletarians are victimized everywhere.
¶ 35-37		The proletariat also undergoes development.
¶ 38-43		This development will precipitate a final collision with the bourgeoisie.
¶ 44-46		The proletariat is the only truly revolutionary class.
¶ 47-48		The proletariat will be free only when the bourgeoisie is destroyed.
¶ 49-51		The proletarian movement represents the vast majority of subjugated peoples.
¶ 52-53		Whereas, the bourgeoisie is unfit to rule.
27%	*II*	*Proletarians and Communists*
¶ 54-59		Only the Communists represent proletarian interests.
¶ 60-62		The Communists' immediate aim is to hasten proletarian acquisition of political power.
¶ 63-69		Communists want to advance the historical process, which always alters property relations.
¶ 70		Communists want to abolish bourgeois private property.
¶ 71-75		Only Communists understand the nature of ruling capital and subjugated labor.
¶ 76-80		Communism has specific views on the meaning of work, human personality, history, and freedom.

Selected Bibliography

THE WORLD OF MARX

ARTZ, FREDERICK B. *Reaction and Revolution: 1814-1832.* New York, Harper, 1963.

BERLIN, ISAIAH. *Karl Marx: His Life and Environment.* New York, Galaxy, 1963.

BRINKLEY, ROBERT C. *Realism and Nationalism: 1852-1871.* New York, Harper, 1963.

COLLINS, IRENE. *The Age of Progress: 1789-1870.* New York, St. Martin's, 1964.

DELFGAAUW, BERNARD. *The Young Marx.* New York, Newman, 1967.

HAMMEN, OSCAR J. *The Red '48ers.* New York, Scribner's, 1969.

HEARDER, H. *Europe in the Nineteenth Century: 1830-1880.* New York, Holt, 1966.

MEHRING, FRANZ. *Karl Marx.* Ann Arbor, University of Michigan, 1962.

PAYNE, ROBERT. *Marx.* New York, Simon and Schuster, 1968.

ROBERTSON, PRISCILLA. *Revolutions of 1848.* New York, Harper, 1960.

SELECTED EDITIONS

BOTTOMORE, T. B. (ed.) *Karl Marx: Selected Writings in Sociology and Social Philosophy.* New York, McGraw-Hill, 1964.

EASTON, LLOYD, and Guddal, Kurt (eds). *Writings of the Young Marx on Philosophy and Society.* New York, Doubleday, 1967.

FREEDMAN, ROBERT (ed.) *Marx on Economics*. New York, Harvest, 1961.

Marx, Karl. *Capital*, 3 vols. New York, International, 1964.

_____. *The Communist Manifesto*. Chicago, Regnery, 1964.

_____. *The Communist Manifesto*. New York, Monthly Review, 1964.

_____ and Engels, Frederick. *Selected Writings*. New York, International, 1968.

SELECTED CRITICISM

BOBER, M. M. *Karl Marx's Interpretation of History*. New York, Norton, 1965.

DUPRÉ, LOUIS. *The Philosophical Foundations of Marxism*. New York, Harcourt, 1966.

FROMM, ERICH. *Marx's Concept of Man*. New York, Ungar, 1961.

GARAUDY, ROGER. *Karl Marx: The Evolution of His Thought*. New York, International. 1967.

HOOK, SIDNEY. *From Hegel to Marx*. Ann Arbor, University of Michigan, 1962.

SPRIGGE, C. J. S. *Karl Marx*. New York, Collier, 1962.

TUCKER, ROBERT. *Philosophy and Myth in Karl Marx*. Cambridge, Cambridge University, 1961.

Index